A Village Murder

JONATHAN ALEXANDER EXAROS

PAGE PUBLISHING, INC.
New York, NY

First originally published by Page Publishing, Inc. 2018

ISBN 978-1-64350-038-6 (Paperback)
ISBN 978-1-64350-039-3 (Digital)

Printed in the United States of America

To my grandfather, Plato Alexander (Exarhopoulos) Exaros.
And to my children—Metani and Alan—this legacy is yours.

CONTENTS

I want to thank the following people for their help and inspiration that led to the writing of this book:

My great-uncle Jimmy (Dimitrios) Exarhopoulos, son of Yiannis. I first learned the details of the double murder of our ancestors from him back when I was a teenager having pizza in the restaurant he owned. I've been infatuated with our family history ever since.

My father, Alexander Plato Exaros, for steering me in the right direction regarding family tree research, my visit to Avgerinos, historical references and about our Greek heritage and culture.

Nick Lingris, for all of his research and translations of articles he uncovered that helped fill in the missing pieces I was looking for. Master Arcenio James Advincula for his expertise in historical weapons and Erik Cunningham for his expertise in geology.

My aunt Jane Dean and brother-in-law Frank Sammut, who helped me with family tree research.

My cousins Pavlina Tari and Christos Tari for their translations and excellent tour guide services when we visited Avgerinos in 2016.

All of my relatives who provided secondhand accounts, family traditions, photos, and articles—especially my aunt Carol Dragstedt and cousins Bessie Vasiliki Trantopoulou, Alexandra Vargiami, Kassiani Exarhopoulos Tsikouras, and Christos Ginis.

Rich Bornstein and my mother, Marge Rubin, for helping me with initial editing and feedback.

My wife, Chanh, for putting up with my obsession over getting this story on paper.

INTRODUCTION

In the central highlands of Macedonia, nestled on the side of a mountain rests the little Greek village of Avgerinos. To get there you must follow the lone highway of E-09, which runs from the east coast to the west coast of Greece through a multitude of well-maintained tunnels that cut into the countless mountains. The main highway is mostly one lane each way. You must eventually depart from this road and venture onto Route 20 where you then embark on a series of winding country roads with switchback after switchback. It is a ride that is guaranteed to make at least one of your passengers come down with motion sickness within fifteen minutes.

From the west coast it takes about three to four hours to arrive in Avgerinos. From the east coast, it is only about two and a half hour's drive. You pass a multitude of fields full of lavender, sunflowers, or corn. Along the side of the road and lining many of the fields are dozens and dozens of bee hives. It makes one think that Greece must be the honey capital of the world. You'll cut through a handful of rustic villages and pass an occasional café or restaurant where you can stop in and sample the local fare.

It feels like the drive takes forever, and of course, the roads are not clearly marked. Even the sign that announces you have arrived in Avgerinos is confusing, as it sits smack dab in the middle of a fork in the road and has no arrow to indicate which tine of the fork you should take. It forces you to take a guess as to whether or not you should go left or right. Go left.

The single road that leads into the village also exits out the back of the little sleepy town. That part of the road didn't exist in the time period discussed in this book. It was built toward the third quarter of the twentieth century and was funded by my great-great uncle Kostas

Exarhopoulos, the wealthy, eldest son of the head of the village, as a donation.

His father was brutally murdered in a field that is just a two and a half hour walk from the center square. Kostas would also make a donation of the clock tower near the entrance of the village. To this day, the loud ringing of the bell annoys the hell out of the owner of the motel, who also happens to be a descendant of the murdered man.

A third donation of an aqueduct was made back when there was no running water in the village. It was a time when the people had to go to a nearby stream to collect their water for washing and drinking, etc. The aqueduct donation was to honor the memory of Kostas' younger brother, Alexander, who was also murdered alongside their father in the most brutal, sadistic, and pointless manner.

When the double murder took place in the late summer of 1928, the roads were unpaved. There were no tunnels cut into the mountains on the main road. Horse or donkey-drawn carts were the only way to get from one village to another, unless you wanted to walk. Avgerinos in the 1920s was a sheep herding and farming community. To this day, shepherding is still a way of life. But back then, it was far more prevalent.

As you enter the village on its only road, you can see the red-tiled roofs and the facades of almost every house. They are built on the mountainside and overlook the deep valley below to your left. Back then, the church used to be one of the first buildings you came to. Built in 1846, it is the pride and joy of the village and serves as the cultural center for most of the family experiences of those that live in Avgerinos.

Amazingly, the church survived the Nazi occupation. Many of the Orthodox churches in Greece were burned to the ground when the Nazis invaded Greece. The Nazis also starved over ten percent of the population to death. But that is for another story.

Walking along the cobblestone streets of Avgerinos during the warm summer months, the mountain breezes blow in the fragrance of lavender throughout the village. It overtakes your senses. In the winter, the place is a ghost town, as nowadays most of the descendants of the villagers who established Avgerinos use it as a summer vacation spot to get away from the hustle and bustle of their city business lives and to reconnect with family. There are still families that live there year-round, though. In the 1920s, living in the village was a life that toughened the heart and the soul and put thick callouses on one's hands and fingers.

The victims of that horrific double murder which took place near the village in 1928 were my great grandfather and his father. It was a crime that the family has only whispered about throughout the generations. I became fascinated with the story ever since I learned of it as a teenage boy. I remember, as a young child, we were simply told that they were beheaded. However, no one ever explained how or why until my Uncle Jimmy recounted parts of this story to me in his Cape Cod pizza restaurant.

Over the years I conducted countless informal interviews of my great uncles, great aunts, parents, grandparents, and older cousins. In 2016, I traveled to the village with my family and interviewed distant cousins who still live there. I received clues and hints and articles from various sources and had them translated into English (I lost my Greek tongue as a child). This book is a culmination of all of that work.

One of the most difficult tasks I faced was in getting accurate accounts of this story. Unfortunately, almost every account I came across, both verbal and written, had many inconsistencies and didn't seem to completely match one another. Some parts of certain accounts didn't make sense. The underlying theme was there, but the exact details would elude me. After piecing everything together that I uncovered or was graciously offered to me, I decided to take my best shot at recreating this story as accurately as I felt comfortable putting into written word.

Aside from some creative liberties I took while writing this book, I am confident that all the names, dates and events in this book are accurate, with the exception of two:

The name Jelalis is a nickname of an individual who our family believes was involved in the double murder. I concealed his real name for two reasons: First, I could find no written account of his involvement in the murders in any article or document. The only account I have are oral traditions, and I didn't feel comfortable accusing someone of this crime without having a written record to back me up. Second, I concealed his true name out of respect for any descendants of his that may still be alive in order to not bring them further dishonor.

The second aspect of this book I cannot assert with a hundred-percent accuracy is whether or not my grandfather, Plato, was a witness to the murder of his father and grandfather.

One might wonder why I hadn't asked my grandfather to provide more details about this tragedy. After all, the first oral tradition that was passed down to me stated that he was at the murder scene at the age of eleven, witnessed the execution of his father and grandfather, then was made to carry the bodies back to the village as a warning to the rest of the family and village.

Could anyone imagine the shock and horror of such an event in a young child's life? It is no wonder that when I asked him once while I was living in his home during my college years, he simply answered, "They were beheaded."

That's all he offered me. He looked down when he said it, and I couldn't bring myself to push him on the issue for something I instinctively knew would have been too painful for him to recount for me.

My grandmother, however, did relate aspects of the story to my father when he was a child. She also gave my mother the same story when we lived with them in Bethlehem, PA, during my father's tour of duty in Vietnam (I was only an infant). I remember as a young man sitting in her kitchen, sipping tea with her when she told me the same thing.

Her story, I can only imagine, would have to be the most accurate due to the strong possibility that her husband may have shared his experiences with his wife. On the other hand, I also had to take into account that people of that generation rarely talked about their trials and tribulations with others, preferring to keep it inside and to move forward with building their lives and raising families. Rare was the luxury of introspection or reflection expressed in those days.

In the end, I decided to combine the most logical aspects of each account and to include the oral tradition that was passed down to me; that my grandfather was present and witnessed the murders. It simply made sense to include it, especially since this was the story that I was raised to believe and the tradition that has had such an impact on our family throughout the different lineages and generations.

This is a story of cruelty, shock and survival. It is a story of immigration and emigration. It is a story I felt compelled to tell to my own children because it is their legacy. However, it should be known that this story is not completely unique to my ancestors. Trace any family lineage back far enough, and you will discover stories of tragedies and survival that will astound our modern-day senses.

CHAPTER 1

Kalliope

December 1911

The girls huddled together in the corner of the donkey-drawn cart as the cold December wind whipped up against the blanket they shared. They were on their way back from school on the two-hour journey it took each way, every day, so that they could receive their education. Out to school at five each morning. Back home by five each evening in time to do chores and help prepare the evening's meal with mother.

Personal reading, studying, and homework would often be completed on the bumpy cart ride home. Otherwise, they would be up late each night by candlelight, straining to read their assignments. This would have to be one of those nights. It was just too cold to do any work in the cart.

With the blanket pulled over their heads, the girls chatted, complained about the cold, and sang songs to pass the time and to get their minds off of the weather. The other boys and girls in the cart, all of varying ages, fended for themselves with their own blankets and talked among themselves as they all passed the time on their ride home from school.

Kalliope and her twin sister, Vangelia (Vangie for short), shared their blanket with Kalliope's best friend, Hresoula (Chrissie). Vangie was the prettier of the twins and drew the most admiration from the boys in their village of Pentalafos. Kalliope didn't seem to mind, though. She had not a jealous bone in her body. She loved her sister, loved spending time with her best friend, Chrissie, and focused on her schooling like no other girl in the *horio* (village).

Kalliope was also known to have a heart of gold. She was thoughtful of others, looked after the younger children in the neighborhood, and was giving of her time whenever asked. People were instantly taken with her and everyone seemed to like the young teen.

Kalliope (right) shown here with her twin sister, Vangie, and another relative. Photo was taken just prior to her leaving Greece, since we know her sister did not immigrate to the USA.

Kalliope stood about two inches shorter than her sister at only four feet ten inches tall. Both girls had slender figures with dark, short hair. They were often teased about their height, but the girls always took it in stride as light-hearted ribbing. It didn't bother them at all. Chrissie, on the other hand, was quite tall for a fourteen-year-old. She was the defender of their clique and tolerated no bullying behavior from any of the boys or other girls in the village toward her friends. She made a great "bodyguard" in that respect. They became lifelong friends.

The day's conversation between the teenagers was focused on their emigration to the United States. Kalliope's father decided to send her and keep her sister, Vangie, in the village to continue her education there. Her father arranged for Kalliope to be married to a man from the neighboring village of Avgerinos. Not really a man, though; he was all of seventeen years of age and she had only met him a few times. He left their homeland of Greece for the United States about a month prior and was by now settling into work and an apartment to establish himself before a marriage could take place. His name was Alexandros (Alexander) Exarhopoulos.

Kalliope's second journey to America would be filled with sorrow born of tragedy. But this first trip would be an exciting one, with the adventure and anticipation that most fourteen-year-old country girls only dream of. It would certainly be difficult for her to leave her beloved village of Pentalafos. But she was up to the challenge, and she was eager to start a new life.

Pentalafos in Greek translates as "five mountains." The views are spectacular from any vantage point within the homes or the village square. The weather in the summer could be brutally hot. Winters caused families to hunker down next to their stoves and fireplaces for sometimes weeks on end. But the spring and autumn seasons were stunningly beautiful and temperate. It was no wonder the villagers took so much pride in the setting of their community.

Kalliope was also comforted by the fact that her best friend, Chrissie, would be coming with her. Kalliope's father managed to convince Chrissie's father to let her make the journey with his daughter. Many of the families at that time were sending at least one child off to make their way in America, so it wasn't too difficult of a task to convince him to let her go.

Throughout their young lives, Kalliope and Chrissie listened to stories and rumors of America from many of the boys and girls in Pentalafos whose older siblings had already made their way across the Atlantic. In the early 1900s, a couple hundred thousand Greek families sent their young men off to the United States. In most cases, they sent their oldest sons with the intention of making their "fortunes," so they would be able to send money back home, secure dowries for marriage, and eventually return to Greece with money for new houses and savings accounts.

Kalliope and Chrissie had been dreaming about going to America for a couple years now. They never thought the opportunity would actually come to fruition and chalked up the dream to fantasy. When the girls found out that Kalliope was being set up to marry a young man from a neighboring village who had already immigrated to America, they couldn't contain themselves.

The girls knew the young Alexander. They previously met him and his family on several occasions, and the families knew each other quite well. The young man's family seemed to be quite prominent and they had a good reputation. Kalliope trusted her parents' decision and accepted she was in good hands for a successful marriage and the beginning of a good, traditional family.

For the young women of Greece, their family role was to marry well, raise children, and keep a home that the rest of the family could be proud of. It was more common than not for the parents of young girls to play matchmaker and set up the arrangements for marriage. Reputation, education, and a strong work ethic were paramount to ensuring the future success of the family.

"What is the name of the village in America your future husband is living in?" Chrissie asked Kalliope. "I forget how to pronounce it."

"New Hampshire," replied Kalliope. "But I don't think it is a village. I think it is a state. The village name begins with a 'man' sound, but I forget how to say it. It also doesn't seem to have a root word that I am familiar with at all."

"Do you think they will have a market there that will be close enough to our home so we don't have to go so far to shop?" Chrissie asked.

"Oh, I have no idea, but I am sure everything will be close. Where we are going has a large community of Greeks. They already have a church there. I know we will make new friends and they will help us. Don't worry, Chrissie," Kalliope assured her.

Kalliope was confident and bold. Too young to travel on their own, and prompted by their fathers, they both lied about their age on their immigration papers and passports. They listed themselves as a year older so that they could make the journey without their parents.

Kalliope and Chrissie immediately started planning and packing when they heard the news of their impending emigration. Both of their fathers felt much more comfortable sending their oldest daughters off across the ocean in a big, hulking ship with the company of each other. This was sure to bring more safety to the girls on their passage as they could look after one another. However, it still wasn't easy to send them off into the great beyond.

The two fathers kissed their daughters on the forehead and gave them a big hug in the foyer of the boarding house the girls were to stay overnight in. The boarding house was just a block off of the docks of Patras. It had taken them twelve grueling days on the backs of donkeys and in one of the coldest winter months to reach the port city. Luckily, they found inns along their journey in the villages and towns they passed through in order to get out of the elements, change into warm, dry clothes, and get something to eat. Still, they felt ragged and exhausted by the time they reached the ocean-side city.

Both fathers signed the girls in for a one-night stay. Tomorrow they would go through the pre-boarding procedures prior to being allowed to board the ship. It was difficult for them to take solace in the fact that after a long journey across the Atlantic, Kalliope and Chrissie would finally settle in a new land. It made it easier knowing that their destination would be a community that was already established for Greeks in a foreign place. Alexander was to find an apartment for his fiancée to share with her girlfriend while they saved the money needed for marriage and to buy homes.

Kalliope carried herself with an air of confidence few girls from the village of Pentalafos possessed. She felt that this trip, her arranged marriage, and the prospects of raising children in the land of milk and honey would satisfy all urges for adventure. She couldn't wait to board the ship. When their fathers said goodbye, they went to their shared room, where they placed their bags. Then, they went out onto the dock to see if the ship they would be traveling on was there. They wanted to see the ship and to get a sense of their transport.

It was a structure larger than anything they ever laid eyes on before. They stood there for several minutes with their mouths agape.

CHAPTER 2

Immigration

After taking in the sights of the busy docks of Patras, the girls returned to the boarding house. The desk clerk directed them to the medical examining office just a few blocks away, and they were told to bring their luggage with them. What they found when they arrived was the first of many long lines the two would have to endure throughout the entire process of immigration from Patras to Ellis Island.

The girls first found themselves in a long line of women and children. The men were standing in a separate line. A few of the steamship employees greeted each woman at the front of the line with a pair of shears. Some of the girls who had groomed long, flowing locks of hair fought back tears as their hair was cut short. Some of them openly wept.

Kalliope and Chrissie's hair needed no trimming. They knew about the requirement for short hair weeks ago, and the girls made a fun event of it by cutting their hair just a week prior to leaving Pentalafos.

They were then directed into shower facilities where they stripped, hung their clothes on hooks, and stood in large stalls to take a disinfectant shower with a soapy substance that wreaked of a pungent chemical no one liked. Kalliope pursed her lips and shut her eyes tight as the soap was sprayed all over her face, head, and body. While the girls were showering, their luggage was fumigated.

Next came quick medical exams. The ship owners took no chances when it came to the health of the passengers. They wanted to ensure every single one of them was healthy and clean. If a passenger with an illness or obvious medical condition slipped through the cracks, it was costly. The authorities at Ellis Island charged the ship about one hundred dollars for every rejected passenger. Plus, shipping the rejected immigrants back home was also on the steamship's expense. It paid to ensure all passengers would pass muster upon arrival on US soil.

Having finished their examinations, the girls finished their showers, dressed, picked up their tagged luggage, and paid for their steerage ticket to the tune of about thirty-five drachmas. For most Greek laborers, it was almost a month's worth of salary. Kalliope and Chrissie's parents came up with the idea that they could save a little money by paying for just one "bed" on the ship that the two girls could share. Kalliope was so small in stature, Chrissie didn't mind sharing at all. They figured it would be no problem, and besides, most of the parents had one or two of their own children sharing the same berth as well.

When they finished collecting their bags, they headed back to the boarding house and were greeted with a small, hot meal before they retired for the evening.

They had trouble falling asleep. Kalliope and Chrissie were simply too excited. The girls chatted about what they thought it would be like to travel across the ocean they had never laid eyes on before. Even the salty air that filled their senses was a new experience, and both of them clamored on about it well into the wee hours of the morning.

Chrissie was awakened on the morning of December 18, 1911, a little before 6:00 a.m. by some stirring outside their door.

"Kalliope, get up," she said as she nudged her sleepy friend awake.

Just then, someone knocked on the door, and it slowly opened. A man peeked his head in and told the girls to follow the street to the loading dock where they would board their ship.

Quickly, the girls dressed, brushed their teeth and hair, packed their sleeping clothes into their bags, and rushed outside to find the street the man spoke about. The sun was just peaking up above the horizon, and the sky was lit up by a bright-red hue.

"Can you believe how many people there are?" Kalliope said to Chrissie.

Hundreds of immigrants, shoulder to shoulder, made their way down the same street toward the docks. Soon everyone stopped, and the girls found themselves waiting in another long line. More waiting.

The girls just kept right on chatting with excitement about what they thought lay before them on this journey. Other would-be passengers glanced over at them in slight annoyance. For most of the adults, it seemed too early in the morning to show such exuberance. Chrissie and Kalliope ignored their stares.

When they finally made it to the entrance of the huge ramp that led upward toward the deck of the SS *Oceana*, they gave the conductor their tickets and were given a single slip with a number on it. Kalliope and Chrissie followed the crowd down into the bowels of the vessel and were immediately hit with the rank odor of sea salt, brine, mold, and must. Neither girl said anything to the other. Their chattering stopped simultaneously. Thinking the same thing at the same time, they pondered as to whether or not they could put up with this inconvenience. The girls would soon find that the odor was to become far worse with each passing hour of the trip.

The girls were handed a tin pail, some utensils, and a life preserver just prior to entering the steerage bay. This is where they would consider home for the next six to twelve days. They were then directed to the bed they were supposed to share after concluding that the number on their ticket matched their assigned sleeping quarters.

The first thing they both noticed was the complete lack of privacy steerage offered. Aside from a few separate washrooms and bathroom facilities, everything was out in the open. The beds, which were constructed of metal, were stacked on top of one another like bunk beds. Each bunk had its own burlap sack stuffed with hay that was to serve as bedding. Although some ships provided a small blanket to each passenger, which they could keep at the end of the journey, this one did not. The girls would have to wear some extra clothes on top of their sleeping clothes in lieu of blankets. Their life preserver was to serve as a pillow.

Their sleeping quarters would also serve as a dining area. In the center of the room were long tables with benches to sit on. The air was immediately sucked out of the room as it filled up with people sharing in this journey. The odor from the rest rooms soon filled the room and became completely inescapable. Not long after the ship pulled from the dock, many passengers became seasick and purged in their beds or on their own clothes. Having little to clean up with, many passengers tossed their soiled clothing overboard when they went on top deck to get a breath of fresh air.

Hygiene was completely overlooked by the SS *Oceana*, if it was even considered in the first place. Their job was simply to get these people to their destination as soon as possible, then return for more. It quickly became apparent to the third-class passengers that they were being treated more like herded animals than like human beings.

Kalliope and Chrissie found that sharing their berth was more difficult than they had originally hoped. However, they made do with what they had. Having only one set of bedding ensured one of the girls always had the hard, metal edges of the bed digging into their ribs and hips as they tried to drift off to sleep. Only one of the life preservers could fit on the bed without the other one falling off every time one of them rolled over in the middle of the night. They took turns sleeping on the inside against the wall of the ship. That was by far the most comfortable position, and whomever had that spot could sleep there without the fear of falling out of bed in the middle of the night.

They arrived in port the day after Christmas, 1911. Although this trip only took eight days, it may as well have been eight weeks. The boredom wasn't half as bad as the odor that hung in the air in steerage after two days of no one bathing, seasick vomiting, dirty baby diapers crumpled in a corner of the room, and the whiffs of urine and feces from the deplorable bathroom facilities. But it could have been worse. The journey could have taken at least four more days, and the seas could have been rougher, with storm surges. They were lucky to be nearing the docks of Ellis Island, and the word of their approach rang out through steerage like a long, expected letter from home.

First and second-class tickets were far more expensive than steerage. Because of this, the shipping company assumed these passengers to be more affluent and, therefore, posed no health risks by carrying diseases. They were quickly shuffled through inspection when they arrived on Ellis Island and passed through customs where they entered the United States of America with little delay.

Kalliope and Chrissie's experience was far different.

First, they were crowded onto a ferry boat in order to cross the bay from the ship to Ellis Island. Immediately, they were hit with a blast of arctic air as they exited the hull, walked across the deck, and descended the stairs onto the ferry. Both girls quickly reached into their bags and pulled out another coat to add a layer to their clothing.

After boarding they were shoved to one side of the ferry where they pressed up against other passengers on all sides of them. They had a chance to look around now. Kalliope stood first on her tippy toes, then decided to stand on top of her luggage to have a look around at the buildings on the shore, the ships in the bay, and the ocean to their right. She couldn't believe the size of the buildings. It was then she laid eyes upon Lady Liberty. Excitedly, she pointed it out to Chrissie who smiled at Kalliope with a deep satisfaction for having made it to their new country.

The ferry began to take its toll on some of the elderly and the young children. It was absolutely freezing and most passengers huddled together to try and keep warm. The lengthy, slow ride to Ellis Island, and the long wait during the boarding and the disembarking process, caused many passengers to get frostbite on their fingers, noses, and toes. Waiting to board, waiting to cross the bay, then waiting to disembark the ferry was intolerable in the freezing conditions, and it added to everyone's misery.

Passengers who needed to relieve themselves found it nearly impossible to get to the restrooms through the overcrowded ferry. Many of them urinated themselves. Even those that could eventually get to the restrooms found the lines also took forever.

Kalliope could hear a woman crying about twenty feet away and was sure that the woman was wailing due to the death of her infant. It sent a shiver up and down her spine. She tried to put it out of her mind.

When they finally landed on Ellis Island and made their way off the ferry, they were provided with a medical inspection card. Kalliope and Chrissie held onto it with dear life while they dragged their luggage, inching toward yet another long line.

The conversations between the girls were stifled by the exhaustion and nervousness they felt as they approached the head of the line. They were emotionally and physically spent. The only relief they could enjoy was the cleaner, fresher air they breathed, now that they were finally out of steerage and away from the odors of the bowels of the ship.

An official-looking woman walked up and down the waiting line and pinned a label onto the lapel of each passenger's coat with wording and numbers neither Chrissie nor Kalliope understood. The line snaked forward, then led upstairs. Standing on the stairway hungry, thirsty, and dragging their luggage up each step proved more difficult than anything else they had experienced so far. The process seemed to take forever just to ascend two or three steps.

When they finally reached the top, they were allowed to move about the large room with some freedom, and they found a place to stand and wait. Both girls used their luggage as makeshift chairs. As they looked around at the other immigrants, it began to dawn on them that they were about to go through another round of examinations.

Kalliope and Chrissie endured four excruciating hours of waiting while doctors made their rounds and inspected each passenger. After each inspection, the doctors marked the card that was pinned to the lapel of each immigrant. Some passengers had chalk marks placed on their backs or fronts of their jackets. The girls couldn't figure out why, and by this time, they didn't care. They just knew they weren't "marked."

Doctors looked into their mouths, checked their hair, examined their hands and feet, and had them bend forward so they could check their spine. The most painful aspect of the examination came when the doctors used a metal rod to lift their eyelids and look into the girls' eyes. Kalliope winced in pain. When the doctor let go, her eyes watered up and she had difficulty seeing as she rubbed her eyes until they felt better again.

The girls both passed their exams.

"I'm surprised we passed," whispered Kalliope to Chrissie. "We both must look like hell," she joked.

None of the immigrants had showered in over a week. Having had to sleep in the same clothes each night for the trip also left each passenger feeling dirty and disheveled.

The girls were then sent to the registry room to be interviewed by a clerk. At this point Kalliope was tentatively separated from Chrissie, and both girls had a slight sense of panic come over them when they could no longer see each other through the crowd. They were placed in separate groups of over two dozen immigrants and a clerk that was assigned to each group began firing out questions while pointing to individual immigrants to solicit the correct answers.

"Do you have money?"

"Do you have a job in the US?"

"Do you have a home in the US?"

"Name?"

"Are you married?"

"Can you read?"

"Do you have a relative living in the US?"

Then the clerk rattled off a series of questions about American History, the flag, and the constitution. Each immigrant was expected to understand at least a little English. All of them looked to be in a state of shock as they tried to focus and reply in correct form.

Kalliope wondered if this process was to ever end.

And end it finally did. Both girls passed the clerks' questions and were directed to a currency exchange counter to change their drachmas for United States currency. They followed the crowd over to the railroad counter, where they showed the ticket agent a piece of paper with the proper spelling of their destination. They made their first purchase with a few of their new dollar bills, and then were led down another set of stairs to the train station.

Luckily, the girls had written directions sent to Kalliope's father by her future husband, Alexander. The directions matched the words written in English to their final destination. They boarded the train and sat down, completely exhausted. The lines, the waiting, the stench of the hull was all over. Kalliope was too tired to think about the end of the line now. All she knew was she wanted to sleep. She wanted to be clean. She wanted a good meal after eating rotten meat, limp, lifeless vegetables, and dank, bland coffee for the past week. She longed for one of her mother's home-cooked meals or at least a decent salad with some vibrant greens and a fresh tomato.

The thirteen-hour train ride to Manchester, New Hampshire, was long, but uneventful. Kalliope spent most of the time drifting in and out of cat naps while she stared out the window at the for-eign-looking homes, factories, modern roadways, and vehicles.

Kalliope and Chrissie were met at the train station by Alexander, who escorted the girls to their new apartment which they would share until marriage could be arranged and paid for by Kalliope's betrothed. Within days she began her new job in the shoe factory and started to make a life of her own in this foreign land.

Over the next few years, Kalliope would become "Americanized," while maintaining her Greek heritage and cultural identity. She would marry, find and make a home, raise four children, lose her fifth in childbirth, become active in her church and community, and would build an internal fortitude that would be vital to her family's existence. It would prove necessary as she would come to face a trag-edy no wife or mother should ever have to endure.

CHAPTER 3

Letters from Greece

About a month before Kalliope immigrated to the United States, Alexander Exarhopoulos joined the masses of Greek immigrants who would come to America to work the factories, send money home to their families, and start families of their own. Alexander was the second oldest sibling of four boys and two girls. He was thin, fair-skinned, and stood about six feet tall. He had a strong chin and held his posture more like the son of an aristocrat than that of a wealthy farmer. He was raised with a strong sense of obligation to his family and placed the importance of honor above all other virtues. He gladly took on the challenge of traveling to America to make his fortune and help his family prosper.

Alexander, in his mid-teens just prior
to immigrating to the USA.

Alexander arrived on Ellis Island November 6, 1911, on the *SS Argentina* and made his way to Manchester, New Hampshire, where he settled in with other Greek immigrants. He traveled to the United States with a few friends, so he wasn't alone on his journey. However, Alexander was still just seventeen years old.

Everyone in the neighboring villages back in Greece kept tabs on how their young men were doing in America. Letters from overseas took a long time to arrive, but were treated like gold when they did.

Alexander's father, Manolis, specifically sent him to New Hampshire because they already had family friends and some distant relatives to connect with upon arrival. He immediately began working in the local shoe factory where many other Greek immigrants had found employment.

The business district was a bit of a hike from the apartment he shared with his friend. Shopping for food and other services was also inconvenient. However, the community he lived in was mainly Greek, and this made it easy for him to integrate into the community and communicate while he worked on his English skills. He became heavily involved in the social fabric of the Greek community and began to make good friends right away. A huge part of this was also his involvement in the Greek Orthodox Church. It was the center of their community and the Greeks relied on it heavily.

Alexander and a buddy of his by the name of Cosmas immediately found an apartment upon arrival in Manchester, located at 136 Chestnut Street. At the rate he was going, he felt he needed about four or five years before he could buy his own home and start his own family. Meanwhile, he would send as much as he could back to Avgerinos for his father to use to improve the village and build him a house there.

Knowing that Kalliope and Chrissie would soon be arriving in Manchester, Alexander used some of his earnings and some of the money he was sent by Kalliope's father to put a deposit down for a small apartment the girls could share. It wasn't too far from his own apartment; about four blocks away, yet far enough to avoid any speculation of impropriety between the couple.

Soon after Kalliope arrived in the States, she and Alexander began to court each other. However, both knew that marriage would need to wait until they could afford a home and were better established, financially.

All of their time spent together was supervised and out in the open within the Greek community. They got to know one another within the venue of church services and other community functions.

Most of the new Greek immigrants that arrived in Manchester immediately went to work at the Hoyt Shoe Factory, which consisted of two main buildings. One of them on Silver Street and the other on Lincoln Street. The conditions weren't the best; the pay was minimal and the distance most employees had to walk to the factory each day was time consuming and cumbersome. It was especially difficult during the harsh New England winter months.

Alexander and Kalliope were patient in their courtship and waited four and a half years before they got married. During that time, they continued to send money home to Greece while managing to save enough to purchase the apartment Alexander resided in on Howe Street. Chrissie and her fiancé, Alexander Nicholas Hassapes married at about the same time and moved into the apartment they had rented for the girls, years before. It all worked out.

Before they moved in, of course they sent word back to their parents, asking their fathers for final permission to go ahead with their prearranged marriage. It was a formality, but it was the right thing to do. The wedding was set for June of 1916.

Although they had waited four years to get married, they wasted no time having children. Their first child, Plato, was born a year later.

It wasn't long after Plato's birth that word spread throughout the community about several shoe factories in Marlborough, Massachusetts, that were looking for immigrants to employ.

After Sunday church services, Alexander and Kalliope found themselves listening in on a conversation between some of the other young parents and elders in the church hall while they all sipped coffee or tea.

George Anastas, a young man who had been in country for well over seven years, was the center of attention this particular morning.

"Everything is in walking distance," said George. He was reading from a letter he received from his cousin in Marlborough. "The houses are on the same block as the factory and most of the homes are owned by Greeks."

"What kind of factory is it?" asked Alexander.

"Another shoe factory! They are looking for more immigrants to make the shoes there. And, get this; they are paying much better than Hoyt. They are also Hoyt's main competition in the market."

George continued, "But that is not all. Aside from the pay, what makes this company even better is the convenience. Everything there is much easier to get to on foot than it is here in Manchester. The kids will have a short walk to school. The markets are close by, and there is talk of building a church there in the very near future. My cousin says the factory working conditions are better, and they treat their employees with respect as valued members of the company."

"How many people does your cousin say they need?" inquired Alexander.

"They are talking about thirty to fifty employees. They prefer people who are already experienced. Apparently, there are plenty of empty houses and apartments for rent nearby, and we will have no problem at all finding a home once we arrive."

Alexander gathered a group of men and women around him and started writing down names of those who might be willing to go to Marlborough and start from scratch again. It was then Kalliope realized that her husband was already becoming a respected leader in the community.

Alexander,
working in the shoe factory.

The increase in pay and the thought of everything they needed being in convenient walking distance was too alluring for many of the young employees. Alexander gave the list of thirty-five Greek men and women to George to pass along to his cousin in Marlborough and asked for confirmation before they committed to packing up and moving there.

Six weeks later, Kalliope pulled out her old suitcase and began packing. The bag seemed like an old friend who traveled far with her from her homeland and was now getting ready for another journey. She laid it on the bed in front of her.

Everything she owned fit neatly in the baggage, but this time she had no room to spare. In fact, she needed two bags for her belongings and for that of her newborn son. What she gathered over the years in the way of possessions since she arrived in the United States now packed two suitcases; new American style clothing, her favorite scented soaps and creams, family photographs, etc. She managed to double her earthly possessions in just five short years.

But she also created a family and was now packing her newborn baby's clothing into a separate bag. Kalliope also helped her husband pack for the journey as well.

She felt herself getting a little nostalgic while neatly folding her belongings and placing them in the suitcase. She was so far from her home in Pantalafos, both physically and emotionally. It seemed almost like a lifetime ago since she lived in the rolling hills of Macedonia. And now she was uprooting herself again in the hopes for an even better life than the one she helped create here with her husband in Manchester.

Kalliope, Alexander, and baby Plato boarded the train at the very same station she came in on five years ago. It felt like almost yesterday. The Exarhopoulos family, along with thirty-three other Greeks, most of whom she had gotten to know quite well by this time, boarded the outbound train for Marlborough. The train pulled out of the station and took them all to their new destination. Once again, Chrissie would accompany her on this trip, and they sat next to each other in the cabin. Another exciting adventure for the girls, who were by now women in their own right.

Kalliope hadn't fallen in love with Manchester. Perhaps she would fall in love with Marlborough.

She smiled to herself as she thought, *Perhaps I should learn how to pronounce it correctly.*

The Howe Shoe Factory, which later was to change its name to the Diamond Shoe Factory, was situated at the end of Howe Street in the center of town. Just beyond the factory property began a series of row homes that lined both sides of the street. They were single, pretty homes, closely built together. The homes were definitely much more attractive than the apartment complexes the Greeks had lived in during their life in Manchester.

One half hour after stepping off the train all thirty-five Greeks, led by George's cousin, made their way past the shoe factory and onto Howe Street to look for apartments and homes in the neighborhood. They were tired and hungry from the trip, but the excitement of finding new quarters took their minds off of their bellies for the moment.

Alexander and Kalliope found a home halfway down the block at 117 Howe Street. It was a small, two-story grey house with a tiny yard. It had no hot water, but it did have a gas burner for cooking and heating. They rented the second floor.

The stairs were rickety to traverse, but the flat was comfortable. The best part of the home was that it was only two hundred yards away from the factory the two of them would be working in. They found a home for their growing family. A couple years later, when the house came up for sale, they purchased the entire building.

The community and the neighborhood exceeded their expectations. Now Alexander and Kalliope just had to make sure they landed jobs in the factory.

Behind the house was a small alleyway called Neil Street. Two blocks up, Chrissie and her husband found an apartment on the first floor of a row home and put down a deposit, then moved right in. The girls were so happy to be so close to one another and were both relieved to have found homes so quickly.

None of them had any trouble becoming employed in the Diamond Shoe Factory. They were welcomed by the company and made to feel right at home. In fact, this company would create a feeling of "ownership" within each employee. The Greeks and other immigrant employees all felt they had a stake in its success.

Alexander didn't take long to become a prominent man in his own right within the Diamond Shoe Factory and within the Greek community. He rapidly moved up into a supervisory position at work and was put in charge of the community fundraising activities to finally get a Greek Orthodox church built in 1925. He was instrumental in helping to raise the $2,500 to purchase the property for the church at the top of the hill behind the school on Main Street. Each Greek family donated $25. In addition, a bank loan for $10,000 was procured, and shareholders pitched in to the tune of $50 each. All of these investments were eventually bought back at the end of construction or donated back to the Greek church and the community.

Alexander (center) with other prominent
members of the Greek community.

Alexander (right) with a friend at what appears to be the
foot of the steps of his home in Marlborough, MA.

It took a year and a half to complete construction, and the church was finally opened in December 1925, just in time for Christmas services.

While Alexander was helping to raise money to build the church, he and Kalliope were also busy building the rest of their family. Their second son, Yiannis, was born a year after they moved to Marlborough in 1918. Their daughter, Athena, came in 1919, and Dimitri in 1921. Although their birth names would appear on each birth certificate, the family anglicized their names and they forever went by John, Tena, and Jimmy. Plato was the only child to maintain his Greek name throughout his life.

The family also made a big deal about John's birthday. The boy was born on the 4th of July. Alexander and Kalliope were truly becoming Americanized and took pride in their adoptive country. They attained citizenship, registered for the draft, and registered to vote.

Unfortunately, a fifth child was still born in 1925 just prior to the completion of their beloved church. The child was a baby girl, who was to be named Kalliope, after her mother. Kalliope took the death of her little daughter hard. It was difficult to put on a brave face during the Christmas celebrations and the grand opening of the Greek Orthodox Church of Saints Anargyroi.

During this entire period, letters from Avgerinos began coming in far more frequently. Alexander's father, Manolis, wanted as much information on his grandchildren as he could get. He longed for the safe return of his son with his new family and often wrote about how wonderful it would be for all of them to reunite in their home village.

Manolis had more acreage than most, a lucrative sheep herding business, several family homes, and plenty of crops in which he kept his family and the rest of the village well fed. He employed most of the village men, treated them fairly, and was looked upon with admiration and respect. He also placed great importance on family and wanted them to be close to him forever, especially now that he was entering old age.

The main problem with his request for Alexander and his young family to permanently return to Greece was they were becoming more and more imbedded in their community in Marlborough, MA. Alexander received a second promotion at work, both he and Kalliope were heavily involved in the church, and their children were going to an excellent school right in their own neighborhood. The children made lots of friends inside and outside of the Greek community. Marlborough was their home. It was the only home their children had known. It was difficult to think about packing it all up to live in Greece.

First family portrait. The two young children are Plato
(left) and baby Yiannis (John). The man in the left of
the photo is unknown, but probably a close friend.

First family portrait with all the children. From
left to right: John, Tena, Jimmy, and Plato.

In one letter to his father, Alexander tried explaining his dilemma in detail. He was sensitive and respectful with his explanation, but Manolis persisted and was rather insistent that his son bring his family back to Greece. It was almost as if Manolis wasn't listening or was ignoring Alexander's gentle pleas.

Part of the problem, Alexander explained, was that the children were all going to school and receiving a top-notch education. Alexander knew that the closest school to Avgerinos was in Tsotyli and that most of the village families only sent their oldest children to school while the younger ones worked the farms and herded sheep. Alexander wanted all of his children to be educated. He thought this would convince his father to allow his family to stay in the United States until his children finished their education.

However, Manolis had an answer for that objection too. He promised his son he would build a school in the village for all of the children of Avgerinos. Exasperated at the letter his father sent informing him of his plans, Alexander threw up his hands in resignation.

"He won't listen," he told Kalliope. "Every objection I bring up he can counter. I'm afraid we must accept the fact that we should return to Greece and live out our lives there. It will be a tough transition for the children, but it is our home country, after all."

Soon afterward, Manolis made good on his promise to build a school, and in 1923 he built one in the heart of the village and sent pictures to his son. It was one less objection that Alexander could use to avoid returning to Greece. He put off discussing the topic as long as he could and, by autumn of 1927, the excuses for staying in America had run out. They decided to return to Greece the following year.

"I really don't want to go," voiced Kalliope. "I have a feeling something bad will happen if we do. And I don't want my children to endure the ride on the ship like we had to."

"What can go wrong?" said Alexander. "My father owns most of the land in Avgerinos. He is a very influential man. He will build us a house there, and now they have a beautiful new school for the children. We can return to our homeland and raise our family with more luxury now than we have here in the United States. Plus, we have more money now to buy better tickets than third class. The children won't have to endure the same conditions we did when we came to this country."

Kalliope was dismayed. She begged her husband not to return to Greece and uproot their family from their well-established home. She shared her objections with Chrissie and the other girlfriends in the community she had made since moving to Marlborough. She was searching for a solution to her problem. She told everyone she knew that something bad would happen if they were to return.

They all dismissed these notions and chalked it up to the fact that she was simply "Americanized" now and was content with sending money each month to her family overseas. She was happy with her life and was well adjusted to the American lifestyle. And her children? They, too, were Americans. Of course, they had no idea how wonderful life could be back in the country of their ancestors' origin. Marlborough was the only home they'd ever known.

Kalliope found she could no longer object to the move after learning that Manolis promised to build a house for the family in the spring of 1928. She had nothing more to say, and she certainly didn't want to risk upsetting her husband any further. She and her family were going to return to Greece. She was going to endure another ride across the ocean and drag her children with her through that experience.

She told herself it wouldn't be that bad, as she was now married to one of the wealthiest men in the Macedonian region that encompassed her home village and that of her husband's. She loved her home country, and although she was happy and felt safe in her new home in America, she gave up on her objections and switched her mindset. She was Greek, and she would finish raising her family in Greece.

Meanwhile, in Avgerinos, construction on the new house was completed with no delay and few problems. It took just seven weeks with the help of many hired hands within the village. Manolis and Alexander's brothers built a home that was not only suitable for his family, but was also one they would be proud to move into. It had a small patio and easy access to the shared outhouse between both

Exarhopoulos family homes. Above the front entrance, Manolis placed a cornerstone with the engraving "1928" on it to mark the occasion.

In April 1928, Alexander, Kalliope, and their four children sat for a group passport photo. It was stamped with travel approval. Alexander and Kalliope gave a two-month notice to the Diamond Shoe Factory. They informed everyone in the church that they were returning in the summer after school was out. They sold the family home on Howe Street and packed as much of their clothes and belongings that they could fit into bags of luggage that each family member could carry.

A week after their children's last day of school, they boarded a train and headed for New York City. They were on their way to Greece. Alexander was reluctant, Kalliope was stoic, and the children were wide-eyed and ready for adventure.

Family passport photo.

CHAPTER 4

School Days

1923

In early 1923, when the spring weather began to break, Manolis turned his attention to the school that was to be built for the children of the village. He wanted the facility to be completed by the time his grandchildren would arrive in a few years to settle in Avgerinos. His dream of having his entire family with him, prospering and attaining their education, would come to fruition.

Manolis convinced the villagers that the children needed a school they could readily access, rather than having to send them to the neighboring village of Tsotyli. The trip there each day took way too much time, and the children had to be up three hours early to get there by donkey, horse, or cart. They were never back in time before dark when chores and farmwork had to be done. Hence, most of the villagers didn't send all of their children to school. In most cases, only the oldest son of each family enjoyed that privilege. The rest of the children had to work the land and family businesses.

Manolis wanted to please his Americanized son and ensure his family was well taken care of. He needed little persuasion that the benefits of a good education and the promotion of the advancement of all the village children was a wise move for the future of their family and community. So, it was a win-win for his family and for the village to build the school. Luckily, the majority of the villagers agreed. They immediately set to work. Everyone pitched in, first by digging the foundation directly across from their beloved Orthodox church.

The old church was built in 1846. It was the pride of the village with hand-carved railings and ornate icons of the saints, their savior, and the Virgin Mary. Village life revolved around the church. Building the school across the street from it only seemed fitting. Avgerinos would have a school they could be proud of, and they would educate all of their children like the more prominent villages and towns of Macedonia. Everyone was excited for the prospects, especially the children.

Manolis, far right, seated with members
of the community in Avgerinos.

Manolis's third son, Pavlos, supervised the dig for the foundation. A group of eleven men went to work early in the morning of May 3. After two hours, the excavators struck something that made a hollow sound. The men quickly removed the dirt only to discover a wooden structure underneath the earth. They began to chip away at the wood and toss this material to the side. When they lifted what they eventually discovered was a huge lid to a tomblike structure, they found multiple burlap sacks stacked neatly along the interior.

The men removed one of the bags, tore it open, and discovered that it was filled with crushed limestone. While they all stood around the pit with perplexed looks on their faces, Pavlos told his younger brother Yiannis to go and retrieve their father.

Yiannis found his father still at home, finishing up his morning breakfast and getting ready for his day. When he informed his dad of the pit they discovered, Manolis suddenly remembered a cache of crushed limestone that he and several other village elders stored in that very spot about fifteen years earlier. They simply forgot about it. Their original plan was to use the limestone for future projects. Crushed limestone was used as a form of cement or agricultural fertilizer when ground into a fine powder. For whatever reason, the men forgot about it and never used the material.

Manolis went with Yiannis to the dig site. He was pleased to find that the crushed stone was still in good condition and that it hadn't gone bad. Discussion among the village men were already in process when Manolis and his son arrived. They were debating how they could split the lime, how many bags each man would take for their families, and how much money each man stood to make.

Pavlos recounted the discussions to his father. Manolis then told the men about the lime pit and why it was reserved in the first place. But beyond that, he said little about how they would divide it among the families. Rather, he walked away from the excavation site and sat down in the shade of a nearby tree to give himself a moment to think about the best course of action. He often did this prior to rendering a decision for the village or for his family.

"This limestone is a gift," said Manolis, as he walked back toward the men. "It was rediscovered under the foundation of our future school. Yes, we should gather it up and sell it. However, I think the money we make should go to the school to fund our project.

"Think of how much better of a school we could make with the money from this lime. It will be far better than what we could get with the amount of investment I am able to make. Think of the desks and books. Imagine the school supplies and the research materials we could buy. But, more importantly, we can afford to hire a good teacher, rather than asking for volunteers from our community to teach our children in their spare time. This is a gift from God. It will help the children and ultimately help our village to become a beacon of education in our area."

It was obvious that some of the village men were not happy with this decision. However, no one spoke out against it because, after all, it was the selfless thing to do. Certainly, no one wanted to appear selfish, and it just made sense. It was immediately agreed upon by everyone that they would take Manolis's recommendation and work toward pulling out the bags of lime, re-bagging it if some of the existing bags were rotting out, and then setting it aside for sale in order to fund their project.

If there was anyone else besides Jelalis who hated the idea and looked upon the decision with contempt, no one expressed their discontent.

Jelalis was the son of Demetris, an employee of Manolis's for a couple of decades. He and his sister, Melina, were born and raised in the village. Melina was very popular and well-liked in Avgerinos. Jelalis wasn't.

Like his father, he worked for Manolis and started doing so since he was a young, teenage boy. He played with Manolis's children, Pavlos, Yiannis, Kostas, and Alexander. He was an accepted member of the community. However, his friends and neighbors knew him to be lazy and deceitful. It was a stigma he couldn't escape, but it didn't seem to bother him. He made no efforts to polish his tarnished reputation.

Jelalis hid his resentment toward the family well. He hated the privilege the Exarhopoulos boys had in the village; their standing in the community and their popularity among the people. He never understood how, by order of birth, Manolis's sons could come into such grace while he and his family were resigned to work for the family and assist in making the Exarhopouloses even wealthier. He blamed his station in life on outside influences, never once attempting to rise above them and better his life.

Jelalis saw his good fortune of finding the lime stripped away from him. He resented the entire notion of building or funding this school because he himself was too old for school and he saw absolutely no benefit to himself. To Jelalis, it was the final straw. He decided he was going to get a piece of this good fortune no matter the cost.

By the day's end, twenty-three bags of lime were pulled out of the pit. Over half of them had to be re-bagged. The men knew there was another day or two's worth of work in order to remove and re-bag all of the mineral before they could begin laying the foundation for the school. Work ended at 5:00 p.m., and each man headed home for a bath and a hot meal.

At around 2:00 a.m. the next morning, while everyone was still fast asleep Jelalis left his home and quietly made his way through the streets of the village. He was careful to use back alleyways to get to the future site of the school. He found it just as they had all left it before the men broke for dinner and to retire for the evening. Shovels were set to the side and the bags lined the dig site near a retaining wall.

His plan was to take just one bag per night. Surely, one bag each evening would not be missed. He imagined how the conversation each morning might take place. He envisioned the men conversing about the missing bag. If anyone noticed, the villagers might just chalk it up to a miscount. He might have a more difficult time on nights two and three, though, and his wheels were already turning about how he could get his hands on just two more bags of lime without the villagers noticing.

He decided to cross that bridge in the morning and come up with his plan while he worked on pulling up more lime bags with the men from the future foundation of the village school. For now, he had a bag of lime to carry through the village to his home in the middle of the night.

The lime bag was heavy. The streets of Avgerinos are steep along the hillside that overlooks the fields of lavender and various crops of corn and currants. From the church, one can see almost every face of every house. They almost seem as if they are stacked up on top of one another when you view them from afar.

Jelalis was twenty-two years old and fairly strong. Like most of the villagers, he was used to traversing the steep hills of the village on foot with little effort. However, trying to carry this huge bag of lime straight up the alleyways and rutted dirt streets of the village was a difficult task for even the heartiest of the village men.

He took ten steps and then set the bag down to rest. Catching his breath, he picked up the bag, took ten more steps, and then set it down to rest once more.

This is taking too long, he thought. *I have to move quickly, or someone might see me.*

He was banking on the fact that his neighbors would all be sound asleep at this time of night. The plan was to be home well before they awoke.

It was dark, cloudy, and the moon was below the horizon.

All conditions are perfect for this theft except for the weight of this damn bag, he thought as he cursed the weight of his loot.

Meanwhile, Manolis's third son, Yiannis, stepped out of his family home to seek the outhouse in order to relieve himself. His eyes were already adjusted to the dark because his home was pitch black inside. Candles were normally extinguished around 9:00 p.m. this time of year, and there wasn't much to do but to get a good night's sleep. Work in the village and the fields began at the crack of dawn. Tomorrow was going to prove to be another tough day of excavation for the new school foundation.

As Yiannis finished his business in the outhouse, he stepped out the door and into the cool evening air before tucking himself back into his pants. Taking a deep breath, he felt the relief of an empty bladder and was just about to step toward his family home to make his way back to bed when he heard a muffled thump. It sounded to him as if something had fallen down on the street below where he stood.

He squinted his eyes in the direction of the noise down the street at a steep angle below him and he saw nothing. His intuition, though, prompted him to stand still and wait to see if he could hear the noise again. A few moments later, he did! Something was moving up the back street toward him and making a strange noise in the process. He stood there, puzzled, staring down the street. He waited.

Fifteen seconds passed and the thump came again. This time, it was closer. It was definitely moving toward him. Yiannis decided to move off to the side of the street, back behind a retaining wall. The stone wall was completely covered with vines and was ready to bloom their spring flowers. Yiannis waited patiently.

Yiannis Exarhopoulos

Thump! There it was again. The same noise. And, once more, moving closer to him. Soon, Yiannis could make out the figure of a man carrying a sack for about ten steps, and then the figure dropped the sack in front of him in order to rest. Instantly, Yiannis knew what was going on. Someone was stealing a bag of lime from the school!

He waited until the figure was within a few feet of him before he exited from behind the retaining wall. He grabbed the man who was clearly startled and they almost fell onto the street before Yiannis gained his balance and held the man up, pulling him close to his own face to get a closer look at who he had in his grip.

It was his friend, Jelalis. The feeling of betrayal and disgust overcame him, and he shoved Jelalis back against the retaining wall.

"How could you do this?" questioned Yiannis in a voice that was not quite loud enough to wake anyone in the nearby homes.

Jelalis thought quickly about what he could say and what excuses he could come up with, but he knew there was nothing that would make Yiannis believe him.

"Please don't tell anyone," Jelalis begged. "I'll put the lime back and we'll forget the whole thing ever happened."

"Put the lime back and I'll think about whether or not to tell the others in the morning," replied Yiannis.

Jelalis tried to shush Yiannis so he wouldn't wake up the sleeping villagers. Yiannis kept his cool but stared Jelalis down and watched him slink off through the streets toward the dig site with his stolen bag of lime.

The next morning, Jelalis was already at the doorstep of the Exarhopoulos home to meet Yiannis and feel him out as to whether or not he had told his family about the incident. Pavlos and Manolis were the first to exit the home and they asked Jelalis why he was sitting on their front stoop. Jelalis simply said that he was waiting for Yiannis.

"Well, go on in," said Manolis. "Yiannis is just finishing up his breakfast."

Yiannis hadn't told them, Jelalis thought. He could tell by the way they greeted him. Had Yiannis spilled the beans to his brother and father, Pavlos surely would have started in on beating him or at least screaming at him right away.

Jelalis quietly stepped into the home and smiled at Yiannis as if nothing was the matter. He was feeling Yiannis out and pleading with his eyes to forget the entire thing. Maybe Yiannis would just let it go, for friendship's sake. Yiannis didn't smile back, though. He finished his morning coffee, put on his work shoes, and motioned for Jelalis to follow him outside so they would not be heard talking in front of his mother, Marika, and his sisters, Vaia and Soultana.

"I'm going to tell the men what happened last night," Yiannis finally said as they stepped outside and onto the street.

"You can't!" Jelalis said with a yell that caught even himself off guard. He immediately looked around to see if anyone had heard him. Then, he spoke in a softer voice. "It will ruin my reputation in the village. Please!" But Yiannis stood firm.

He walked on ahead of Jelalis toward the dig site. That's when Jelalis grabbed Yiannis in a bear hug in some vain attempt to stop him. Yiannis shook side to side to try and get some room for his hands to move and then kicked backward and downward, stomping on Jelalis's shin and instep. Jelalis screamed out in pain, holding his leg and backing away from Yiannis.

As Yiannis turned toward him, Jelalis swung and caught Yiannis square on the side of the temple with his fist. Yiannis staggered back, composed himself, and stared at Jelalis with a look of disbelief. He could take no more.

The two men locked up in a choke hold on each other. Unfortunately for Yiannis, his back was to the decline of the street and Jelalis ended up on top of him. Down the street the two men rolled. Elbows, knees, and skulls scraped along the cobblestones as each man struggled to gain the upper hand. Fingers scratched and gouged at each other's necks and faces.

Once again, Jelalis ended up on top of Yiannis, and that is when Yiannis pulled Jelalis's face closer to his and proceeded to bite the nose clean off of Jelalis's face!

The taste of blood and gristle in Yiannis's mouth immediately caused him to gag, and he quickly spat the entire nose out of his mouth directly in Jelalis's bloodied face.

Jelalis let out a primordial yell and again backed away from Yiannis, holding his face. Blood spewed out onto the street and poured down along his chin and neck. As Jelalis held his hands to his face, the blood poured down his forearms and onto his shirt and pants.

By now several villagers approached the scene of the altercation. Jelalis ran back to his home as Yiannis collected himself. His adrenaline ran so high that he didn't quite yet feel the scrapes and bruises that covered his arms, legs, neck, and face.

He wiped as much of the blood away from his face as he could with the front of his untucked shirt and told the villagers that witnessed the end of this two-man battle to follow him. He then marched down the street directly toward the excavation site of their future school with a procession of village men behind him.

The shocked look of the men's faces when they saw the amount of blood on Yiannis seemed to freeze them right in their tracks for a moment. They gathered around him to inquire about what had occurred.

Before Yiannis could repeat what happened, more and more villagers began to show up to see what all the commotion was about. Yiannis decided to get as many witnesses as possible to hear what had happened, so he told everyone to gather up their families and come down in front of the village square so he could tell everyone together what had transpired.

Fifteen minutes later, almost every villager with the exception of Jelalis was standing in a circle in the village square around Yiannis, who was still on an adrenaline high from the incident. His father and brother Pavlos tried to calm him down.

Yiannis told the villagers about the previous night's incident; how he caught Jelalis stealing the lime and how Jelalis tried to stop him from telling everyone before they started work on the excavation this morning.

He could see the disgust and surprise on the villagers' faces. Trust within the community was paramount to village survival and success. The people of Avgerinos worked together to build everything and to provide for all their needs. If the trust is broken, the entire village suffers.

Jelalis would never recover his honor within the community now. The villagers knew it. Jelalis knew it. He would always be known as the liar and thief of Avgerinos.

What made matters even worse for Jelalis was the fact that his entire nose was bitten off in his altercation with Yiannis. Even after Jelalis' face would heal, there was very little he could do to hide the hideous disfigurement that was now his face. It would be a constant reminder to everyone around him as to what he had done. He would probably never marry. Women would cower from his mere appearance and children would be sure to point and poke fun at him. Jelalis lost his face, both figuratively and literally.

CHAPTER 5

Battle on the Ridge

He couldn't let it go. How could he? The festering wound on his face which still dripped of pus and blood was a constant, painful reminder of his disgrace. He couldn't sleep on his back at night because the blood dripped down the back of his throat. Sleeping on his side only helped him to fall asleep and stay asleep for a little while before he was awoken by the puddle of fluid on his pillow turning cold against his face. Sleeping on his belly was impossible. He could feel his pulse in the wound and it pounded painful reminders of his disfigurement with each throbbing beat of his heart.

He bandaged up his face the best he could with the help of his mother. Breathing became incredibly difficult, and he had to rely solely on his mouth for that function. The fluids dripping down his windpipe caused him to cough and gag throughout the day.

He also found eating to be quite difficult and a challenge as he gagged and slightly regurgitated with every bite he attempted. His mother said nothing to him while applying his daily first aid. She was embarrassed and disgusted with his theft, like the rest of the residents of Avgerinos. Her shame was magnified by the sorrow she now felt for the future of her son.

How am I going to live like this? he thought.

It didn't appear that there was any hope of it getting any better. How could it? Even after his wounds healed, he would be forever known as the man with a hole in the front of his face. He would have to live with this for the rest of his life.

It was during this painful healing process that he came to the conclusion he would make Yiannis and his family suffer the way he and his family were now suffering. The very thought of it consumed him and temporarily took his mind off his pain. He occupied himself by running different, vengeful scenarios in his mind and played with the fantasy until he no longer thought of his disfigured face.

The plan came together for Jelalis the second morning after his fight with Yiannis. Earlier that morning, he climbed to the top of the hill above the village to distance himself from his neighbors and to be alone with his thoughts and anger. Fifteen minutes of solitude and introspection passed when he gazed down the hill to his left. He couldn't believe his luck when he noticed Yiannis walk past the village cemetery into the field below. Yiannis was driving his father's sheep for the morning hours.

"Perfect!" Jelalis said to himself out loud.

He ran back to his house and took his father's M1903/14 bolt action rifle from the mantle in their living room. Excitement overtook him as he came to realize he would have his revenge much sooner than he imagined.

Jelalis was never known as a great thinker. His plan was completely short sighted and he never gave consideration to how he would live in the village or how he would explain his deed after murdering the youngest son of the most prominent and beloved man in Avgerinos.

His intention was to kill Yiannis and perhaps hide the body, but there was no time to think about hiding anything right now. He made haste to intercept Yiannis. His desire for retribution clouded his judgment and he rushed headlong into his plot to kill the son of Manolis while no one looking.

After retrieving the rifle, he was careful to slip out the back of the village, over retaining walls, through backyards and neighboring gardens so no one would see him leave with a rifle in his hands. He ran back up to the top of the hill, then sat down to catch his breath.

As he quieted himself, he scanned the fields below for any sign of movement. At first, he saw nothing. But soon he spotted something moving in the culvert between the two main fields down by where the water runs off the hill from the village when it rains.

Sheep! He knew Yiannis would not be far behind the ewes. He quickly made his way down the hill toward the field. He cut across to the east and decided to hide in a small cove of trees and make his ambush from there. After about twenty minutes of hoofing it through the tall weeds, he settled into the cove behind one of the largest trees he could find. Looking down toward where he last saw Yiannis, he waited for his prey, knowing Yiannis would be headed straight toward him.

Unfortunately for Jelalis, the sheep popped out of the woods further down the valley than he expected. He was going to have to place a long shot, about two hundred plus yards. During his years of hunting, Jelalis never shot at anything that was more than a hundred yards way. That didn't seem to matter to him now, as his quest for revenge consumed him more than reason possibly could. He understood a little about windage and elevation and figured he would just aim his rifle a little above Yiannis's head to meet his target of hitting him in the chest.

Aiming was far more difficult than he thought it would be. The open iron sights of his rifle were shaking and bouncing all over his line of vision. He had a difficult time focusing from the tears that still formed in his eyes due to the pain inflicted on his face by Yiannis. He could hear his heartbeat pounding in his chest and felt it in his throat. He couldn't believe how fast his heart was racing. With his heart rate elevated so, it magnified the pulse of pain in the outer rim of his severed nose.

"This is more difficult than killing a deer, by far," he said to himself in almost a curse-like manner.

He grew frustrated, but he took a deep breath and decided on timing the bouncing iron sights when it would be directly over Yiannis's head. He squeezed the trigger and the shot rang out and echoed throughout the valley.

Yiannis hit the ground after he saw the explosion of wood in a tree just a foot away from his belly and then heard the echo of the gunfire come from across the fields. He looked up from the ground at the tree next to him and saw splintered wood, green and fresh as it stood out plain as day among the rest of the scarcely sparse trees and saplings that checkered the gully and separated the fields his father owned.

Who the hell would be shooting and hunting at this time of year? he thought.

Then it hit him. He realized immediately that this was no accident. He was being shot at!

"Damn it, Jelalis!" Yiannis whispered to himself. It could be no one else.

Yiannis had spent two years in the Greek military after he finished the 11ᵗʰ grade. He wanted to take after his father, Manolis, who years earlier supported the "National Ideal" and fought bravely on the side of Greek Rebel forces when Yiannis was just a child. He had early childhood memories of how his family and the entire village provided material goods in the way of food and money to support the struggle at that time. Yiannis was a seasoned veteran, and now his training was about to be put to the test.

The sheep already scattered further up the gully toward the field Yiannis was originally driving them toward. He did some quick calculations based on the starburst wound in the tree where the bullet entered the trunk. He slowly raised his head out of the reeds just enough to get his bearings on where his attacker might be.

The very first thing he noticed was the cove all the way across the field.

Two hundred yards away! What an idiot! Yiannis thought.

Fortunately, the gully Yiannis was laying prone in was fairly dry and led almost directly to the cove of trees, where he wagered his attacker must be still lying in wait in.

He pulled out his MAS-1873 revolver, one of only three pistols in the entire village. Handguns were a luxury in Macedonia. Those that owned them either had enough money to afford them or kept what they were issued during prior military engagements when they served in the military. His father was one such farmer, and Yiannis and his brother Pavlos took turns carrying it whenever they herded sheep.

He then began a slow, long crawl at the bottom of the gully toward his attacker.

This is going to take a while, he thought. *I must exercise patience.*

Jelalis wasn't actually sure if he hit his intended target or not. The slight puff of smoke, his watering eyes, and the pain in his face that he felt from the recoil of the rifle made him lose sight of Yiannis after he pulled the trigger. As he gazed across the field toward where Yiannis was last seen, all he knew was that Yiannis no longer stood where he last saw him. He could see the sheep run up the edge of the gully and into the field to his right. But there was no Yiannis.

Did I hit him? he wondered.

He decided to wait. Ten minutes. Fifteen. After twenty minutes his patience wore out. He pulled the bolt back on his rifle and chambered another round. He slowly stood up and began making his way across the field. His eyes remained fixed on where he last saw Yiannis when he took his shot.

Jelalis's steps were labored, careful, and quiet. He dreaded every moment of it. He was often compelled to look down to avoid stepping on a dried twig. The last thing he wanted to do was to alert his intended victim of his approach. He couldn't bear the thought of taking his eyes off of where he last spotted Yiannis, but he had to be sure to make no noise. He quickly raised his gaze to look in that direction again. Closer and closer. One hundred seventy-five yards away. One hundred fifty yards away. One hundred yards away and closing.

Meanwhile, Yiannis had crawled for a considerable amount of time without looking up to see where his attacker might be. He didn't want to give away his position. However, it was now about forty-five minutes into his crawling and, frankly, he got tired of it and needed to stretch. Slowly and quietly he brought himself up into a crouched position, taking great caution not to stick his head up above the reeds just yet. Then, with the slowest of movements, he made his way up into a squatting position just high enough so that the top of his head was still below the top of the reeds. He looked toward the cove of trees. Nothing. Then, just as he was about to lay down and continue his crawling routine again, he caught a figure out of the corner of his eye to his left, standing in the middle of the field.

His attacker! And the predator was looking toward where Yiannis's position used to be when the shot was made.

Yiannis wasn't spotted. The attacker had no clue that Yiannis was off to his left. He stared at the man with the rifle, watching him slowly stepping toward the position where Yiannis initially stood as prey to this assault. The distance between the two men was only about sixty or so yards away.

Much too far for a pistol shot, thought Yiannis as he stared at the man who was tracking him.

It didn't take long to recognize the attacker. His movements, mannerisms, and the bandage around the middle of his face confirmed his initial instinct. It was Jelalis!

This was the final straw. *Jelalis is a dead man!* Yiannis thought.

He got down on all fours and started crawling toward Jelalis's position. Yiannis was about to turn his predator into prey.

He knew he had to move quickly, but still needed to maintain absolute silence and not give his position away. Jelalis was walking, although slowly, toward Yiannis's original position and would eventually create even more distance for a pistol shot to be accurate or effective. Yiannis had to close the distance if he was going to shoot Jelalis and take him by surprise.

Crawling through the thicket was no picnic. His knees ached with every stone that imbedded itself into his knee caps and shins. His hands and forearms began to turn raw. After a grueling twenty minutes of crawling over stone and dirt, he decided to rise up and have another peek. This time Jelalis was just thirty yards in front of him. His attack could now begin.

Yiannis slowly stood up. Jelalis still didn't see him. He was facing the other direction and definitely more focused on what was in front of him than on his surroundings. Yiannis got his circulation back into his feet and legs and hands, took a deep breath, pointed the pistol and yelled as loud as he could, "Jelalis!" Then Yiannis bolted and ran directly toward him.

The shouting of his name shattered the silence of the quiet, empty field and startled Jelalis. He accidentally fired his rifle into his left foot, blasting away his first two toes. Wincing in pain, he spun toward Yiannis who was already firing his revolver in Jelalis's direction. The second shot hit Jelalis square in the shoulder. Jelalis fumbled with the bolt of his rifle and tried racking another round into the chamber. However, Yiannis's fourth shot went through Jelalis's arm and grazed his rib cage. Jelalis fell flat on his face. He was still alive but lay perfectly still. He closed his eyes, held his breath and waited for what seemed to be an eternity for Yiannis to put another bullet into him.

Yiannis kept running and came up upon Jelalis as he lay there in the weeds. Blood was everywhere. It was seeping from his face from under the bandage on his nose. He could see the exit wound in the back of the shoulder and the hole his bullet made in Jelalis's right arm. On top of that, he could see blood seeping out of his boot where Jelalis shot his own toes off.

He was dead, Yiannis decided. He kicked the rifle away from Jelalis and then picked it up. Yiannis was out of bullets anyway and was thankful that his shots were accurate enough to hit the mark at least twice. He decided to leave the body where it lay and head back to the village to gather the men and tell them what happened. For now, he was feeling like the luckiest man on earth. He celebrated his good fortune with a whistle as he climbed over the hill and back toward Avgerinos

CHAPTER 6

Body Vanish

Although the villagers had already shunned him and looked upon him with shame, when they heard of his attack on a beloved son of Avgerinos, it was difficult to show pity when Yiannis informed them that Jelalis's body was lying in a field waiting for retrieval.

"At least Jelalis won't have to live through life in disgrace and shame," some of the villagers murmured to themselves. "He would meet his maker and pay the ultimate price for his treachery."

They now had a duty to go and collect the body and at least give him a proper burial. Most of the men in the village wanted to participate in the collection of the body. After all, in the mundane lives of herders and farmers, there was little excitement like this. A shootout in the fields between two of their neighbors was something not to be missed, even if it was only to witness where it took place and to see the body of the loser.

However, Manolis decided to take only about a third of the men, pleading with the rest of them to continue their work on the school. He wanted it completed by the end of the summer and there were crops and sheep that needed tending.

"We need to have the foundation completed before planting season is in full swing," Manolis asserted.

Most of the men begrudgingly went back to work on the foundation. The younger boys of the village followed behind the retrieving party at a distance. They were just too curious not to be somehow involved in all the excitement of an attempted revenge killing.

Yiannis led the men to the site of the shootout. All the while he kept repeating his story about how he escaped certain death and snuck up upon Jelalis and killed him. He was proud of his prowess, and he now felt vindicated and invincible. He felt like a celebrity. His military training finally paid off. The years of training certainly served him well, and he was now being treated as a hero to the people in the village. For the first time, it seemed he was getting more attention from them than all three of his older brothers.

Yiannis couldn't believe his eyes. Upon reaching the spot where the shootout occurred, he looked but there was no body. Jelalis was gone! Manolis and Pavlos started rattling off questions in rapid succession.

"Are you sure you killed him?"

"Didn't you check his pulse to make sure he was dead?"

"Might there have been someone else with him that you didn't see?

"Perhaps dogs or wolves carried the body off?"

"Are you sure this is the spot?"

Pavlos looked down at the ground and searched for signs of blood. There was plenty of it. This was definitely the spot where Jelalis had been laying.

The blood trail led down toward the gully, where Yiannis had spent so much nerve-racking time on his belly crawling toward his attacker. The gully was dry, and they followed the blood trail easily for a couple dozen yards or so. Then the blood trail veered off toward a damp creek bed, and the blood trail began to fade in the tall grass. It became more soupy and wet as they traversed it in the direction they knew Jelalis would have had to travel. Occasionally they would find a foot print or a drop of blood, but the signs were dwindling. Jelalis was using the creek to make his escape, and there was no telling how far he would go before he exited the ravine to seek some shelter. He could have turned out of the creek bed anywhere.

Pavlos Exarhopoulos, second from the left.

"Jelalis can't be long for this world," Yiannis tried convincing the men. "I definitely shot him twice, and the idiot blew part of his own foot off. Those wounds will surely cause him to bleed out. Plus, he has his ugly face to contend with. He will bleed out. I'm sure of it."

"I hope you are right, my son," Manolis stated. "Personally, I'm not comfortable giving up right now until we recover the body."

"He's dead," Yiannis assured the men. "Let the wild dogs take his body."

Yiannis was hungry and his nerves were shot from his ordeal in the field. He and several of the men returned to the village after Yiannis insisted that Jelalis would surely perish if he wasn't already dead.

However, his brother Pavlos wasn't convinced. He and a few of the other men decided to continue their tracking despite Yiannis's confidence. They did so for over three hours before they, too, turned back for the village, conceding that Yiannis was probably right. If Jelalis could survive until night fall, he wouldn't make it through the cold night of the mountain and would surely die of hypothermia.

Jelalis couldn't believe his luck. *Why hadn't Yiannis finished me off?* he thought.

His gamble of playing dead paid off, but he certainly wasn't out of the woods yet. The wound in his arm was excruciatingly painful. His ribs stung. He was hobbling around on a foot with only three toes, and his face felt like it was on fire.

He crawled his way into the gully that Yiannis had come from, then hobbled as fast as he could down the stream. He tried to stay in the water so as not to leave a trail. He knew his blood would be everywhere, but he hoped as it fell into the water it would dissipate and leave no trace. He passed the splintered tree where Yiannis stood, where Jelalis thought he had killed him. He cursed his misfortune at having missed Yiannis and then he just kept on going.

Once he passed the second set of rolling, overgrown fields, he decided not to break for the hills but to keep going. He had no idea to what length the villagers, and especially Manolis, Yiannis, and Pavlos, would go to track him down. He had to keep going until at least dark set in. He found a stick among the trees to help him in his hobbling along and continued his escape.

When the sun started to fade over the far mountain to his left, he stopped and looked around. He was so thirsty he couldn't stand it anymore. He squatted where he stood and leaned forward to take a good long drink of the water he stood in. He swallowed water, mud, and some of his own blood. It was a relief. He was covered in his own blood and sweat and, for the first time, he paused to take inventory of his wounds and to see just how bad off he was.

His foot was a waste. He didn't even want to take his boot off yet. He knew he had farther to go to find shelter, and he didn't want to contend with the pain of having to put the damn boot back on. He felt his pants for his pockets and was surprised to find his handkerchief. He pulled it out and stuffed it into the open hole at the edge of his boot in an attempt to stop the bleeding.

Jelalis then turned his attention to his right forearm. He found a perfect hole between his ulna and radius. The bullet had passed perfectly between the two bones. He didn't have another bandage to stop the bleeding. He thought of tearing a piece of his pant leg off to tie around the wound, but he found he had no use of his right hand. The bullet must have damaged the muscle or the nerve. He couldn't even make a fist.

He decided to ignore the wound for now. He pulled open his shirt with his left hand to check his ribs. For some reason, this was the most painful of all his wounds. It appeared as if the bullet only grazed him there, but it also broke a rib in the process. He could clearly see the wound in his side and noticed a bit of white bone glistening with the fluid that oozed from there. He decided to just close up his shirt and continue on his way.

Fumbling with his left hand to button up the last top button to keep out what he knew would be a cold evening, he took a moment to look around at his surroundings. Up on the hill to his right was a fire! A campfire!

Surely these people would take me in, he hoped.

They would have no idea of his crime or attempted murder and he could make up a story about how he was attacked. The people in the camp would certainly have mercy on him with his nose-less face and his three other wounds. He knew he looked like hell.

Will they take pity upon me? he pondered.

He gingerly rose to his feet. The short rest he took caused his muscles to lock up and everything seemed to become far more painful now. Just sitting for the brief amount of time he allotted himself to check his wounds seemed to have stiffened him up quite a bit.

After about a dozen steps, he found his cadence, slow and labored as it was. He limped and hobbled across the field toward the base of the hill where the campfire could be seen. It was about halfway up the hill. He made his way up the slope and toward the fire. It was dark now, but the light of the campfire led the way for him.

As he approached, he found five men sitting and chatting in a language he immediately recognized as Albanian. Strangers from a neighboring land in *his* land of Macedonia. It was a risk coming up to these men, but what choice did he have? He waived at them. All five men instantly stood up. Two of them pointed rifles in his direction. One of them drew a yataghan sword.

Jelalis could see the Albanians also had two mules tied off to the side of their camp. He raised his left arm above his head.

"Don't shoot! I am wounded and I need some help."

When the men got a good look at the pathetic individual that stood before them, their defenses came down a bit. Then they looked beyond him and searched for others who may be in pursuit of this sad looking creature.

The Albanians spoke Greek with a thick accent. Jelalis found communications with them wasn't difficult at all.

"What happened to you?" asked one of the Albanians.

"Someone tried to murder me," replied Jelalis. "I've been tortured and shot, but I managed to escape from the nearby village. I'm in need of help. Can you help me?"

The Albanians tended to Jelalis's wounds and provided him with some food and bedding next to their fire. He spent the next three days and nights camping with these men in the same site. They helped nurse his wounds, and he slowly began to gather his strength. His recovery was fueled by his hatred for the Exarhopoulos family and the village he left behind.

Jelalis found living the life of a nomad in the woods and mountains suited him. He spent the next four years living in the countryside, stealing food and finding shelter where he could. He bounced from group to group of Albanian bandits wherever he could find acceptance. However, his time with each of the gangs was fleeting, and he soon moved on to be by himself or to find another group to temporarily latch onto.

Eventually he came upon one of the most notorious Albanian gang leaders in all of Macedonia. This leader and his group of brigands in particular would put Jelalis's knowledge of the surrounding areas of Avgerinos to good use. They would also capitalize on his facial disfigurement as a way of striking fear into the hearts of their intended victims.

CHAPTER 7

Albanians

Throughout the early 1920s, several individual Albanian bandits and gangs moved down through the mountains of Albania and into the villages and surrounding countryside of Macedonia and Northern Greece. Some of the groups even made it as far south as Lefkada and Athens. They competed with each other for control over the land, exacted money in the form of "taxes," forced farmers to pay a stipend of crops and mutton, and held shepherds and farmers hostage for ransom money.

Travelers and traders were often the victims of their attacks. The gangs had a stranglehold on the people and competed among each other to expand their territory.

In the fall of 1923, soon after the school was completed in Avgerinos, two half brothers bearing almost identical names, Christos Forfolias and Christos Laventis Forfolias, were among the many Albanian bandits to make their way into the Greek countryside. To avoid confusion where they grew up, Christos Laventis Forfolias was simply referred to by family members as Leventis. His brother would maintain his first name and both men built separate reputations and formed their own gangs throughout intersecting Macedonian territories.

Before Christos Forfolias crossed the border into Greece, he worked as a muleteer and often as a local constable in his home town of Kafaloxori. Running mules, he found, wasn't quite as lucrative as wielding the power of a corrupt constable.

He often took bribes from criminals who were on the run from authorities and harbored them in his home while acting on false pretenses as if he were searching for the same thieves. Eventually his activities were uncovered and the authorities began to question Forfolias. With his suspicion aroused, and fearing an impending arrest, he ran off with several of the bandits he developed a relationship with. He turned to the life of a brigand from that point onward.

Christos Forfolias's first crimes were simple burglaries and petty theft. Although he was uneducated, he was bright and had a talent for manipulation. When the commander of Larissa, Major Stathoulopoulos sent a posse of four men from Forfolias's home town to capture him, it took just three days for Christos to corrupt all four of the posse's men. Instead of arresting Christos, they joined his gang.

Christos Forfolias
Picture taken when he was a constable in his hometown of Kafaloxori.

Stathoulopoulos was furious. He revoked the posse's deputy status and issued new warrants for the arrest of the entire Forfolias gang. It would take two full years before all of the men were taken into custody by April of 1927.

Laventis's introduction into a life of crime was quite different. His baptism of violence came in the form of an honor killing. Honor killings were fairly common in small Albanian towns at that time. If a woman rejected a man's attempt at courtship, the embarrassment to the man's ego would be so egregious that he might end up killing the woman and her entire family.

While Laventis's half brother was fleeing the Albanian gendarmes and crossing the border into Greece, Laventis had his eyes on a neighbor's young daughter who lived just four houses down from his family home. She was only thirteen and her parents felt she was not quite mature enough for a courtship.

Laventis persisted. Yet she thwarted and rejected the older, aggressive Laventis and was obviously not interested in the young man. When she told her parents of the harassment, they went to Laventis's home and politely asked his parents if they could talk to Laventis to convince him to leave their daughter alone. They said she needed more time to grow up, and they promised the family that they would revisit a proposal for an arranged marriage in a couple of years when she matured.

Laventis was mortified. Most of the townspeople of Kafaloxori found out about the entire ordeal as rumors spread of the conversation between the two families.

Laventis's embarrassment over the rejection was unbearable. He was flush with anger over the negative attention and looked at the girl's parents' request as more of a scolding that was beneath a man of age twenty-two. He felt as if he was being treated like some child.

Two nights later he snuck into the girl's parents' home and killed the entire family, including the girl, with a short dagger.

Having massacred the entire family, he ran away and escaped into the northern mountains of Greece, where he met up with his half brother, Christos. The two men decided to split up and create their own separate gangs to cover more territory.

"There's plenty to go around," said Christos. "These peasants have enough for us to live off of very well over the next two decades if we choose."

Although Laventis avoided capture and eluded the authorities for years, Christos wasn't so lucky and was captured just a year later. While his half brother languished in jail, Laventis went on an extortion and killing spree that would claim the lives of several farmers and a couple of their wives.

Commander Stathoulopoulos was at his wits' end. He was completely at a loss for how to capture the remaining gangs and bring them to justice. Finally, he appealed to the court prosecutor and devised a plan by which they would pit rival gangs against one another in the hopes of a "divide and conquer" tactic to rid the area of the Albanians once and for all.

Incredibly, they hatched a plan with Christos Forfolias and his partner at that time, Giorgos Trandos, to stage a jail break. Stathoulopoulos allowed the bandits to go free under the guise that they would let the two men operate their gang in the same area that Laventis was known to frequent.

Stathoulopoulos lied to Forfolias and told him that he could have free range of the area surrounding Kozani, so long as they kept within the confines of that region. The only thing Stathoulopoulos demanded in return was a promise that Christos would kill, capture, or set up Laventis for an ambush. If he could do this, Christos could have Laventis's area and be free to conduct his "business" as he saw fit.

The plan was naive and ill conceived. Stathoulopoulos had no idea that Laventis was Christos's half brother because Laventis was only known to the authorities by his first name. No one knew the two were actually related. In addition, Stathoulopoulos ignored the lessons of the past and did not take into consideration Christos's talent for manipulation.

Christos and Trandos agreed, of course, to the conditions set forth by Stathoulopoulos. The jailbreak was staged, and within a week Christos and Laventis joined forces and began one of the worst seasons of crime and murder the Macedonians had ever seen.

In addition to the half brothers' newly created partnership, they were soon joined by a third relative; a nephew by the name of Evangelos Maras. Maras crossed the border a year prior to join up with his uncle Laventis.

When Christos set eyes upon his young nephew for the first time in years, he was delighted. Maras was no longer the scrawny teenager he remembered him to be when Christos left Albania so many years ago. Maras was now a young man, and Christos was overjoyed to have another family member as part of their gang. After all, who better to watch your back during their excursions than your own flesh and blood?

With the creation of their new gang, the Forfoliases became emboldened, and their crimes became more frequent. They robbed people in broad daylight, extorted money from the village heads, and stole sheep and other livestock at will without any fear of reprisal. By the second month of 1928, they had committed five murders and dozens of hostage-takings and extortions.

By this time Christos, Laventis, and Maras added two more men as their main companions in their criminal enterprise. Vlach Ondos was the first and was a childhood friend of theirs from Kafaloxori. Ondos heard about the success the Forfolias gang was having and decided a life with a gang was much more alluring than the life of a shepherd. By this point, he was only with the gang for two months and already was considered a valuable asset and a member of their "family."

Their newest member was none other than Jelalis. Jelalis was accepted into the gang when the brigands came upon him wandering between villages. Forfolias figured he could be quite useful in their campaigns due to his knowledge of the region. In addition, his facial disfigurement would be perfect as a means of intimidation.

Like most people who first met Jelalis, Christos Forfolias's initial reaction was one of disgust at the open hole that lay dead center in the man's face. But Forfolias felt he could use a man like Jelalis for several reasons. First, his appearance would add to the shock and fear the gang could perpetrate upon the people they intended to victimize. Just seeing this man, Forfolias thought, would cause people to cringe and cower. Second, Jelalis was familiar with the area and could speak the language fluently. Third, Jelalis was an outcast among his people and no longer had any loyalty, affection, or pity for the people they would be stealing from. He was a perfect addition to the gang. Together, they established a reputation of being the most ruthless of Albanian gangs to terrorize the villages from the border of Epirus and beyond.

Jelalis had been wandering from village to village in an attempt to find some sort of acceptance and usefulness. He was able to join several different gangs throughout the years and he took part in the banditry that would plague the mountains of Macedonia. Several times he tried to influence the gang leaders to visit his home of Avgerinos with the intention of seeking his own revenge against the Exarhopoulos family. But, the hierarchy within the gangs didn't lend itself to be influenced by a mere Greek peasant with a hole in his face. The gangs had their own agenda, and Jelalis was just along for the ride.

But the Forfolias gang was different. Even before he had taken Jelalis into his gang, Forfolias had already set his sights on Avgerinos, Pentalafos, Dafni, and other villages of the mountainous region in that area.

In June of 1928, the gang had kidnapped two young shepherds near Anaselitsa, which was only a four-hour walk from Avgerinos. Forfolias sent a letter to the young men's parents informing them that if they did not receive a ransom of 100,000 drachmas within seven days, the shepherds would be slaughtered.

At the time, a captain of the gendarmes by the name of Papaconstantinou had been working tirelessly for a few years to eradicate the bandits from the region through capture, trial, incarceration or banishment. During this particular kidnapping, Papaconstantinou finally caught up with the gang and nearly had them surrounded.

However, Forfolias and his men evaded capture once again. One of the shepherds they were holding hostage managed to break away from the gang during the gang's escape, but the other one was found dead in an open field the following day. His throat had been slit and his body stripped of what little he possessed.

By this time Forfolias was getting a good understanding of the terrain. He and his half brother and nephew were foiling capture at every turn. Some of his other gang members weren't always as lucky.

Vlach Ondos was captured twice for petty thefts, spent a few weeks in jail, and was released. Another extended member of the gang to be captured and interrogated thus far was a conscripted Greek shepherd by the name of Sarakatsani, who often offered refuge to the gang for payment and frequently went out on their excursions to steal from travelers.

Like most shepherds, the bandit life was just far too lucrative and attractive for Sarakatsani to turn down when the opportunities arose. By now, Captain Papaconstantinou and his patrols knew each member quite well and were building profiles on the entire Forfolias gang, issuing warrants for their arrest and soliciting the locals as posse members to track them down.

When Forfolias set his sights on intended victims for extortion, his MO was to distribute letters to all the prominent farmers and heads of a particular village, explaining exactly what he wanted. Now that they had a Greek in their gang, Forfolias dictated each letter to Jelalis, who wrote down the demands in their language so that there could be no misunderstanding.

The stamps above were used by the gang on the letters sent to those they extorted from. The one on the left is Christos Forfolias's and the one on the right is Laventis's.

The letters informed each head of each village that Forfolias was now in charge of the area and was offering "protection" from competing bands. Their compensation would occasionally be of sheep, crops, or money, depending on the season. In this case, Forfolias was levying a tax of 250,000 drachmas. The letter further mentioned that the bandits would be more than willing to sacrifice the children of the village if they did not receive the payment within seven days of receiving the letter.

The next step in Forfolias's plan was to find a delivery boy who would deliver each letter. In the case of Avgerinos, Jelalis knew exactly who they could go to.

"I have someone in mind to deliver your message," Jelalis said to Forfolias.

"My old supervisor, George Konas, is the shepherd supervisor and works for Old Man Manolis, who is the wealthiest man in all of Avgerinos. Konas has a cabin on the outskirts of the village. His cabin will be a great location for us to hide out in and to get out of the elements for a while."

Forfolias nodded. Jelalis was proving to be an invaluable member to have in his gang.

When the men approached the cabin a few days later, Konas was quite surprised and intrigued to see Jelalis. He hadn't seen him in over five years. Rumors were widespread that the "man with no nose," had joined various Albanian gangs and was stealing money from villages far and wide. Everyone from Avgerinos knew that it had to be Jelalis, but no one bothered to follow up on the claims and no one seemed to care. He was an embarrassment and a blemish on their village and they wanted nothing to do with him.

In addition, most of the gang activity appeared to be far enough away not to affect them. When Konas laid eyes on Jelalis for the first time since the fight between Jelalis and Yiannis, Konas knew he was in the midst of a ruthless Albanian gang.

"Jelalis, we thought you were dead. How are you faring, my friend?" Konas tried putting on a brave face despite the danger he assumed he was in. He acted as if he was happy to see Jelalis while masking the terror that shot through him as he came to realize the seriousness of his current situation.

"Very well," replied Jelalis. "We have come into the area because we want to offer the good people of Avgerinos the protection of my boss, Christos Forfolias. He has the strongest influence in the mountains and is helping to keep robbers and thieves away from our families and farms."

Laventis and Maras paid little attention to Konas and began to check out the cabin and the surroundings to get a feel for the building and what comforts or food may be awaiting them inside.

"We want you to join us in our efforts to save Avgerinos from those that would do it harm," continued Jelalis. "Boss Forfolias pays handsomely to those that help us. Will you be open to his request?"

Konas was in a bad position. He couldn't say no. *Perhaps there may be a silver lining to this predicament,* he mused.

Self-preservation kicked in. "I will be happy to assist Boss Forfolias. What does he require of me?"

Konas was given the handwritten letter and was promised a nice financial reward when the taxes were paid to the gang. Without objection, Konas agreed to deliver the letter to his boss, "Old Man Manolis."

Over the months that Jelalis came to live with the gang, he often spoke to Forfolias about the wealthy land owner. Manolis was very robust and energetic for a man of seventy years. A former military man in his youth, he saw quite a bit of action as a member of the Greek rebel forces. He was intelligent and had a keen eye for business. He now owned much of the land surrounding Avgerinos, and his sons were rapidly making a name for themselves as well.

Manolis's third and fourth sons, Pavlos and Yiannis, followed in their father's footsteps by joining the military. His oldest son, Kostas, was a popular businessman who kept himself busy between the seaport city of Salonika (Thessaloniki) to tend to his apartment complex and other city business dealings there.

Manolis's second son, Alexander, immigrated to the United States after graduating from school to make his "fortune" there. He regularly sent money back to his family in Greece for savings and to invest in a future home. Manolis and his wife, Panagiota rounded out their large family with two young daughters, Vaia and Soultana. The entire family was respected and well liked in the mountain community.

Before George Konas was sent off on his errand, Forfolias and Jelalis questioned him about the Exarhopoulos family. It had been years since Jelalis left the village of Avgerinos in disgrace while escaping the wrath of Yiannis and his family. Certainly, some things had to have changed in that time.

"Old Man Manolis's second son, Alexander will be returning from America with a lot of money," Konas told them. "I hear he has purchased two expensive gold watches he is bringing with him. One of the watches will be worn by Alexander and the other he purchased as a gift for his father."

"This is interesting," replied Forfolias.

"Manolis has built a nice home for his returning son with the money that was sent back from America over the years," Konas continued. "Plus I know that the oldest son, Kostas, is doing quite well with his businesses and apartment complex in Salonika. He often returns to Avgerinos bearing gifts, and he throws his money around to fund parties and family events around the holidays."

Forfolias turned to Laventis, "Perhaps our tax of 250,000 drachmas is not nearly enough for this family. Maybe we should consider an increase in our demand?"

"Let the letter stand for now," replied Laventis. "We can always increase the tax next quarter."

They sent Konas off with instructions that he was to give Manolis seven days to comply and then collect the money directly from Manolis and deliver the tax to the Forfolias men.

Konas delivered the letter to Manolis the following day. Manolis had no way of knowing that copies of this same letter were distributed to others in the region. He figured he was the only one being targeted for this extortion. All he knew was that his employee, George Konas, was standing in front of him with a letter of demand.

"I fear for my life if you do not comply, boss," Konas pleaded with Manolis. "I think these men should be taken seriously."

Manolis carefully read and reread the letter several times. With each reading, he became more and more incensed.

"These Albanian dogs don't know who they are dealing with," Manolis said out loud to himself. Not only did he take umbrage to the extortion, but the last thing he needed now was to have his son, Alexander, and his family be frightened and filled with regret for having returned to Avgerinos.

"Let's keep this letter between the two of us," Manolis said. "Tell no one about it. I can deal with these bandits if and when they come. How many are they?"

"I only saw five," replied Konas. For some reason, he decided not to tell Manolis that Jelalis was one of the members of the gang.

"Where are these Albanians now?" Manolis asked Konas.

"I don't know," he replied. "They went off and said they would return to my cabin for the money sometime in the near future."

"Go back to your cabin and continue to work," he instructed Konas. "If these dogs return, simply tell them that you gave me the letter and that I would comply. But tell them I stated I am not the wealthy man they think I am. Tell them I may need more time to get that amount of money saved up. We will stall them, Konas. I can't have this problem now that my son is returning with his family from America."

He then sent Konas on his way.

Manolis had no intention of capitulating. What he did do was to take extra precautions when traveling his property throughout the countryside. He began to bring along one of his hired hands as a bodyguard during his time afield and would also often bring at least one of his sons with him wherever he went. His chosen bodyguard was Athanasios "Thomas" Vargiami.

Thomas was a large, muscular man, a field worker and a jack-of-all-trades who could mend or build just about anything. He drove sheep, worked the fields, supervised various projects, and had a reputation in Avgerinos as a "tough guy." He was also known as an excellent hunter and owned his own firearms.

Manolis paid Thomas a little extra to shadow him as a bodyguard whenever he went into the fields to check on his crops, livestock, or survey the land.

Jonathan Alexander Exaros

"Are you concerned about your safety?" asked Thomas. He had worked for Manolis for many years, but this was the first time he was asked to accompany him as an armed companion.

"I hear rumors that there are bandits about. I'm just taking precautions," Manolis replied.

Manolis put a lot of trust and faith in Thomas. Everyone knew him to be a man of integrity. Thomas slung his Gras M-1874 single shot rifle over his shoulder and began to carry it everywhere the men went. He didn't question the rumors any further, and Manolis never let him in on the letter he had received from the Forfolias gang.

CHAPTER 8

Betrayal

Six weeks passed and Forfolias still hadn't received his reply from Manolis. The other prominent village leaders in the area had all capitulated and made their payments. The only village family who never replied were the Exarhopouloses.

Forfolias sent Konas back to visit Manolis two times during that six-week period with his renewed demands. Each time, Manolis replied that he needed more time. Forfolias's patience was running out.

"It is time to move on the village of Avgerinos and exact payment," Forfolias told his men.

Jelalis was elated that the old man didn't respond to the demands of the letter. Even if Manolis made a payment of 250,000 drachmas a few times each year, it would never meet Jelalis's quest for revenge. He wanted more.

In the middle of August 1928, Forfolias returned with his gang to the cabin of George Konas. The cabin was about a two-hour walk from the south end of the village. It sat at the top of a steep slope along a hill overlooking the valley below. It was more of a shack and served as a temporary home away from home for the shepherds who worked for Manolis and herded sheep in the fields surrounding Avgerinos. It was large enough for eight men to sleep comfortably, had a small kitchen area for meal preparation, a fireplace, and a long table with benches for the shepherds to eat together after long days in the fields. The floorboards creaked and spewed dust up through the cracks when you walked on them. None of the shepherds really cared much about that. It was a roof over their heads and it certainly was better than sleeping outdoors.

As the gang approached Konas's cabin, they could see it was currently unoccupied. They entered the cabin and made themselves comfortable inside the dwelling, happy to be out of the elements for the first time in quite a few days.

It wasn't until about four hours later that Konas and his shepherds arrived. Konas was immediately put off by the intrusion of the strangers in his cabin. He had already given up his cabin several times to the Forfolias gang. He gave in to their request to deliver their messages to Manolis and made promises not to reveal their whereabouts if questioned by the authorities. The gang was becoming a liability to Konas, and he still hadn't received a single payment for his efforts.

Konas turned to his shepherds. "Wait outside while I speak with these men."

The shepherds begrudgingly sat in the yard, smoking and talking among themselves as Konas went inside to talk to the gang.

Jelalis initially did all the talking.

"Hello, George. We are back, as you can see. We were hoping that Old Man Manolis would have given you our payment to deliver to us. Tell me, what is the status of payment?"

"Manolis says he needs more time. I have pleaded with him several times to give up the money for your tax, but I think he is not taking your demand seriously. He keeps complaining that he is not the wealthy person you think he is. He says he is happy to pay a tax, but that he needs more time to gather the funds."

"This is unfortunate," lied Jelalis.

"Konas, my friend," injected Forfolias. "Our plans have changed. I will pay you handsomely for information on where Old Man Manolis might be in the next few days. We want to approach him when he is away from the village so that we can all talk in private. Perhaps we can talk some sense into him."

Konas was intrigued at the prospect of finally procuring a payment for information. Plus, he really didn't want to end up a victim of a ransom gone "bad," like the shepherd in Anaselitsa he recently heard about. News traveled throughout the area about the gang that killed a shepherd in a field there just two months ago. Konas assumed he was in the presence of the very gang that committed that horrific murder. He dared not ask them about it and considered himself lucky that these men were not taking *him* hostage.

"No need for me to seek information. I actually know where Manolis will be over the next few days," said Konas.

"Really?" asked Laventis. "And where is this place?"

"Old Man Manolis is planning to build a new farmhouse and barn for his family to raise crops of corn and to breed more livestock. He and his American son have visited there frequently in the last week or so to survey the land and to lay their plans. The area is known as Tsativi. It is only about a half-hour walking distance from here. I can take you there so you can see," explained Konas.

Jelalis knew Tsativi well. He remembered driving sheep into that area.

"I know of the place," he told Konas. "I can lead Forfolias to the area myself."

"Your boss, Christos Forfolias, thanks you for your time," Forfolias said to Konas. "We may be back in a while to bed my men down for the night. I'm sure you won't mind extending us some more of your hospitality for one more evening?"

"Of course not," Konas said, begrudgingly.

Forfolias pulled out a wad of bills from his pocket and gave Konas thirty-five drachmas. It was a little more than Konas made in a month. He stuffed the bills in his pocket, thanked Forfolias, then went back inside the cabin while the gang made their way toward Tsativi to have a look around.

Konas's cabin may have only been a half-hour walk to Tsativi, but Jelalis knew it was more like two-and-a-half hours' distance from the village. It would definitely be secluded and a perfect area for him to finally attain the revenge he had sought over the past five years.

Upon arrival, Forfolias had a good opportunity to survey the area and the lay of the land. He thought to himself that this was the perfect setting to capture the men and to force them into payment.

"I have seen enough," Forfolias stated with satisfaction. "Let's return to the cabin of George Konas and get a good night sleep. We have work to do in the morning, and nothing is going to happen here this late in the afternoon. We will return in the morning. Hopefully the Exarhopoulos men will be here like Konas stated."

When they returned to Konas's cabin, Konas was alone. He sent his crew of shepherds out to drive sheep for the next few days in order to get them out of harm's way and to protect them from any implication that may come if something bad were to happen to the Exarhopoulos men. Plus, Konas didn't need witnesses to his dealings with the Albanian gang.

"Where the hell did the shepherds go?" demanded Forfolias. He was none too pleased the shepherds were gone. "What if they tip off the authorities and tell them that we are here?"

"I apologize, boss Forfolias," replied Konas. "I assumed you didn't want them around and I never told them who you are."

Forfolias bit his tongue and decided not to reprimand Konas further. They would have to exercise extra caution now, and he knew they couldn't stay at Konas's cabin for too long.

He took no unnecessary chances. All five of the Forfolias gang were to take turns on watch duty in a field that overlooked the trail leading to the cabin. The night passed without incident.

In the morning, Forfolias sent Vlach Ondos out to the hill that overlooked Tsativi as a scout. He was given instructions to come back to the cabin when the Exarhopoulos men arrived to survey and work their property.

Ondos reached the hilltop a half hour later and sat down in the tall grass. He lit a cigarette and relaxed in the warm morning sun while he gazed down at the valley below.

By pure coincidence, a patrol happened to be moving through Tsativi that very morning. Ondos hadn't even finished his smoke when he noticed the patrolmen moving in the field below him, and he immediately recognized Papaconstantinou who headed the patrol.

Shocked at seeing this patrol of eight men and thinking that the authorities were already on to their plan, Ondos panicked. Without thinking, he fired off a warning shot to alert the gang in Konas's cabin which was just a little over a mile away.

Immediately, Ondos wished he hadn't pulled the trigger. The patrolmen would probably have just walked on by without noticing him. They weren't even headed toward the cabin of George Konas in the first place.

The patrol was on top of Vlach Ondos before he could collect himself. After a brief struggle, they easily subdued him and began questioning Ondos as to why he fired a shot.

"I tried shooting my dog who is sick. I wanted to put him down," said Ondos, making up the story on the spot and secretly taking pride in his quick thinking.

"There is no dog around here, and if it was sick, how could it have gotten away?" replied Captain Papaconstantinou.

"Wait a minute," the captain continued. "I know you from somewhere, don't I? I've arrested you twice before. Your name is Vlach Ondos!"

Ondos looked down. He knew he was in trouble.

"This man is definitely associated with the gang activity in our area," Papaconstantinou said to his posse. "A few other gendarmes and I caught him on two other occasions stealing crops and sheep. He is not to be trusted."

He then turned to Ondos. "I thought I warned you twice to leave this area and go back to Albania where you belong," shouted Papaconstantinou. "Why have you not heeded my warnings?"

He was quite irate and red in the face. Ondos simply looked down at his feet and didn't say a word.

Papaconstantinou's patience ran out. He ordered his men to tie Ondos to a tree, face first, with his hands tied as if hugging the giant trunk. He bent down and picked up a stick that he could easily wrap his entire hand around. The whipping commenced.

Ondos bore the first few blows without a sound but began screaming after the fourth stroke. At the seventh or eighth, Ondos was more than willing to give up information.

"My gang is up at the cabin of George Konas," he said.

"What gang?" demanded Papaconstantinou.

"Forfolias," Ondos replied as he winced in pain from another blow to his back.

"Why is your gang back in this area?" demanded the Captain.

"They are just passing through," Ondos lied.

He made no mention of their plans or conspiracy to attack Manolis and his family. Ondos figured he could give them a little information on the whereabouts of the gang, knowing full well he just warned the bandits with the shot of his rifle. Perhaps they got away, he thought. Better yet, Ondos hoped the gang might rescue him from capture.

The patrol left Ondos tied to the tree and headed up the hill to Konas's cabin. When they arrived, they kicked in the door, rifles at the ready, but the bandits were gone. Only Konas was found at the kitchen table, calmly eating a meal as if nothing had happened.

Konas thought briefly about giving up the bandits. However, his main concern was that if the patrolmen did not find and capture the gang, the gang would return and then he would be on the wrong end of their retribution. Harboring the Forfolias gang might continue to be quite profitable for him if he played his cards right.

"Where is the Forfolias gang?" Papaconstantinou questioned Konas. "We know that they were here. Do not lie to us."

"I'm so relieved you came," lied Konas. "Forfolias and his gang were here overnight and they made me put them up and feed them here. I am so thankful you have arrived because they terrify me. When they heard the shot, they ran off and told me not to tell you where they went."

"Well," replied Papaconstantinou. "Where did they run off to?"

Konas lied again. He sent the patrolmen into the woods toward a completely different direction than where Forfolias and his gang were headed.

"They ran that way as soon as they heard Ondos's shot."

Konas sent the patrolmen west. As a result, Papacaonstantinou and his patrol turned up nothing. They returned to the cabin a few hours later, but Konas was already gone. Konas decided to catch up to his shepherds and spend the night in camp.

At this point, Papaconstantinou grew suspicious of George Konas.

"Write down the name of George Konas," he told one of his subordinates. "We might have a need to come back to Konas for more information. I don't trust that man."

The patrolmen returned to the tree where they left Ondos tied. He was still there, of course, and they took him into custody to a nearby village where he was temporarily locked up. A few days later they transferred Ondos to Kozani, where he was to be put on trial.

CHAPTER 9

Plato

August 21, 1928

Plato stepped through the front door of his new house and into the fresh country air of Avgerinos. It took two months to get used to being away from his schoolmates, his neighborhood friends, his home in Marlborough, and his life as a natural-born American citizen. At age eleven, he was the oldest of his three siblings and was already mature beyond his years. He was bright, an insatiable reader, and had a knack for numbers and figures.

Plato also had a passion for running. He loved the adrenaline rush he got from running up and down the hills of Avgernios. It became a new challenge for him while sprinting from home to home or playing ball in the village square with the other boys. The hills were daunting at first. But he quickly got used to them like everyone else who lived there.

Back home in Marlborough, his father and mother spent hours with their children, reading and re-reading letters from their grandfather, Manolis. Alexander often spoke to them about Avgerinos and wove a tapestry of descriptions that made the mountains of Macedonia seem like paradise. He also instilled in them a sense of overwhelming pride about their Greek heritage, the history of their ancestors and what it meant to be an Exarhopoulos.

But Alexander and Kalliope's children were also Americans. They already had a home they loved. Their parents had steady work and a career in a shoe factory of suburban Massachusetts. Plato, John, Tena and Jimmy loved their hometown and cherished the school they attended.

Plato finished up his fifth-grade education in early June and was excited about moving into junior high school in the fall. That excitement and expectation was soon washed away with the news that they would be immigrating to Greece.

When Plato first laid eyes on the school in Avgerinos he had difficulty hiding his disappointment.

"This little building?" he said to his mother. "It could fit inside just one of our classrooms back home in Marlborough!"

"Hush now," Kalliope scolded him. "Don't judge the school by its size. Your grandfather spent a lot of money and hard work to build this facility just for you and your siblings."

Out of respect, he tried hard to keep further criticisms to himself and he secretly wondered if he would receive a challenging enough education in this tiny, three-room school.

Like most Greek boys growing up in America, Plato attended "Greek School," which was provided at the Orthodox Church in town. Although he was born in the US, his first language was Greek. He was fluent in the language and could read and write in his parents' native tongue well before he entered grade school. He relished the letters his grandfather sent from Macedonia. He memorized the descriptions of the land, the church, the cousins and uncles and aunts who lived there.

John seemed to share Plato's interest in the letters and their father's descriptions. Tena and Jimmy were too preoccupied with their lives as young children to show interest beyond the storytelling of a faraway land.

During the middle of Plato's fourth grade school year, he noticed the change in his grandfather Manolis's letters. His writings seemed more focused on requests for the family to uproot and come to Greece. Plato couldn't seem to put his finger on it, but he became a bit apprehensive about the whole idea.

He was comfortable in Marlborough. This was his home. It was the only home he had ever known. He couldn't imagine moving to another place. He was attached to his school, his friends, and his familiar neighborhood streets. Yet there was something about the village of Avgernios that also called to him. The letters from his grandfather and the descriptions of his father made the village seem as if he already lived there once. It was a part of him. It was in his blood.

It was a difficult move and a challenging transition, but Plato kept an open mind and soaked in the adventure of the journey and the surroundings of his new home. He complained little when the family packed up everything they had at the end of his fifth-grade school year and headed off to New York City to board the ship that would take them to Europe.

They arrived in Avgerinos late June of 1928. Having been in the village now for two months, Plato was finally getting used to the way of life, and he relished in the beauty of his surroundings. He often played in the fields of currants with his new friends. The aroma from the lavender fields would often blow in from the westerly winds and fill the village with the sweetness that could normally only be experienced by placing one's face deep within a bouquet of the finest flowers. He never grew tired of it.

He became friends with most of the boys. He knew he was much more educated than they were, and he took pride in his knowledge and the edge he had attained in his worldliness. He became sort of a celebrity among them. They all wanted to know about America. He enjoyed this newly found popularity and accepted his nickname with pride; "American."

Plato was also treated more like a man by the elders of Avgerinos than he had been by the elders of Marlborough. Boys and girls had to grow up much quicker here to work the farms, drive the sheep, and assist in building the farm structures. On the third day after his arrival in Avgerinos, he already took part in some of the repairs and finishing upgrades of the new school his grandfather built for the grandchildren. It was exciting to be a part of the maintenance of *his* new school, even if it was a tiny building compared to his school back in the United States.

He took another deep breath as he looked out over the horizon at the sun, which was already just above the horizon on this beautiful summer morning. Today was a little different. His grandfather and father were taking him along on a two-hour ride in the countryside to survey a valley and to determine a perfect site for the future extension of the Exarhopoulos farm estate. His grandfather was the prominent man in the area and owned most of the surrounding fields and land. It was an honor for the oldest grandson to be invited at such a young age to go along for the ride and discuss the future of their family. It made Plato feel as if he was a contributing member and an adult in his own right.

CHAPTER 10

Innocence: The Third Murder

Thomas Vargiami helped Plato into the back of a donkey-drawn cart. Manolis had kept Thomas close by for quite a while now, and it was becoming a habit to have him by his side throughout his daily routines. It was especially comforting to Manolis to have Thomas around when he ventured out of the village into the countryside to check on his crops and livestock.

To Plato, it almost felt as if they were going on a family picnic. He sat up in the hay and hung his arm off the side of the wooden beams as his father and grandfather climbed up in front. Thomas placed his rifle into the cart, then hopped up into it and sat down in the hay across from Plato. Then, they were off.

Thomas gave Plato a wink and a smile. Plato smiled back at Thomas and then looked out at the scenery as they drove up the hill, past the last house.

They continued on the road beyond the cemetery and then back down the other side of the hill toward the sheep pastures, where they picked up the trail that lead to Tsativi. Plato and his father, Alexander, had no idea that they were driving through the area where Jelalis had taken a shot at Plato's Uncle Yiannis five years prior. The story of the altercation was also something that wasn't talked about much.

Although it was already getting quite warm, it was a beautiful day and they enjoyed the ride with the breeze that sometimes hit their faces. The trail wasn't well maintained. Few people came this way. Shepherds often drove sheep in this area. Otherwise, the only humans to traverse the area was the occasional villager in search of firewood to collect for the winter.

About an hour and a half into their two-hour trip, Thomas smacked his own forehead and informed the Exarhopoulos men that he had forgotten to pack water and the food they were to have for lunch into the cart.

"I'm so sorry," said Thomas. "I think I left it all on the counter of my kitchen while I went outside to get the donkeys hitched to the cart. I completely forgot."

"Maybe we should all turn back," Alexander stated.

"Nonsense," said Thomas. "I'm the one that caused this problem. I will just quick-step back to my house, pick up our lunch and water and quick-step it back here. It won't be a problem. Plus," Thomas turned to Manolis, "I know you really want to spend time with your son and grandson to show them the land and future home of your family."

Thomas hopped off the cart, picked up his rifle, and began a slow jog toward the village. "I'll be back in a few hours by lunch time," he shouted as he made his way back up the trail. He waved at Plato and Plato waved back.

Had Thomas known of the threats made to Manolis by the Forfolias gang, he never would have left him and his family alone in the fields of Tsativi that morning. Had Alexander been aware of the threats, he never would have brought his son out of the village and into the countryside.

Manolis didn't object to Thomas's insistence on walking back to the village to get the food and water. He hadn't been threatened lately and rumors circulated indicating the bandits had vacated the area a month ago. His guard was down.

When Manolis, Alexander, and Plato finally reached their destination, it became quite apparent why Manolis wanted to build their new family farm in this area. The rolling fields appeared easy to maintain. The view was fantastic, and the fields were already cleared of trees. Very little had to be done. They could build their homes and barns and immediately begin to plow the land next year in the spring. It was perfect.

Emmanuel (Manolis) Exarhopoulos

As they walked around, discussing their plans on where each structure should be placed, they heard a voice in the distance.

"Hello!"

They could see several men coming down the hill toward them, one of them waving. The Exarhopouloses had no reason to feel alarmed from the body language of the approaching strangers. They waved back, thinking they were either farmers or shepherds just passing by. The Exarhopoulos men went about their business.

Manolis kept an eye in their direction and could see the men getting closer. He could now see that there were four of them.

For a brief moment, a panic shot through Manolis that these men might be the Forfolias gang. He shook off the notion, reminding himself of the rumors he recently heard that the bandits had moved on toward the border and into Epirus. He told himself that these were just passersby.

"Relax," he mumbled to himself.

As the strangers got within about two hundred yards, Manolis yelled out to them, "Are you lost? Can I help you?"

No reply. The men just kept on coming. Now Manolis could see that one of the men had a rifle in his hands. The other three had yataghan swords. The rifle was nothing uncommon for famers and sheep herders. But the yataghan swords threw up an immediate red flag to Manolis. He didn't want to alarm his son or grandson, so he tried to remain calm. He could talk his way out of this if these fellows were, indeed, bandits. He was used to exerting his influence, and in the worst-case scenario, he could simply promise to pay the men off and then seek out help from the authorities.

"Greetings, my friends. How can I help you?" Manolis said as the men got within just yards of his family.

The man in the center, obviously the leader of the group, spoke at last. "Are you Old Man Manolis, grandpa?"

The accent was a clear giveaway. These were definitely Albanians.

"Yes, that is me," replied Manolis with a frown on his face.

He took umbrage to being called, "old man." It seemed more of an insult than a term of respect. His face became flush, and he tried to conceal his panic by remaining stoic.

"I am Christos Forfolias."

Manolis's heart rate shot up so high he could hear it pounding in his ears. He felt it throbbing in his fingertips. As the bandits came within a few feet of the Exarhopoulos men, Manolis immediately recognized Jelalis.

Manolis was struck by how ragged-looking Jelalis appeared. He had definitely aged, was disheveled and had lost weight. The hole in his face was unmistakable. Over the years the scar tissue hardened around the edges of his gaping wound. It gave a more fierce look about him.

Jelalis said nothing. He didn't have to. Both Manolis and Jelalis knew that by Jelalis's mere presence here among these bandits meant some sort of exacted revenge for what Manolis's son Yiannis had done to him years ago. Manolis's fear briefly gave way to anger at Jelalis, but he didn't want to escalate the situation—not with his beloved son and grandson present.

"You must be illiterate, old man," said Leventis. "We sent you a letter months ago letting you know who was in charge of the area security. Yet you don't bother to come and make payment to us for our generosity."

"I believe I sent word back that I did not have enough money to pay and that I needed more time. Tell me what it is you want and I will get it for you right away. We want no trouble," Manolis replied.

"You are a liar!" shouted Leventis. The sudden outburst caused Plato and his father to startle. It was then that it became quite clear to Alexander and Plato that they were in immediate danger.

Leventis spoke again. "You think we are fools? Perhaps you need a lesson as to who is in charge in this valley."

"Father," said Alexander as he pulled Plato close to him. "Who are these men?"

"Shut up," snapped Forfolias. "No one has given you permission to speak yet. Is this one of your sons, old man?" Forfolias directed the question toward Manolis.

"Yes. This is my son, Alexander."

"Ahh," said Forfolias as a smile came across his face. "This is the rich American we've heard so much about."

"We are not wealthy people," said Manolis. "We are merely sheep herders and farmers."

"Liar!" shouted Leventis.

Maras, who held one of the yataghan swords, kept quiet. He casually started circling around the back of Alexander in order to surround the Exarhopouloses and to minimize any thought they might have of making a run for it.

"Calm down," Forfolias feigned admonishment toward Leventis. "There is no need for hostility here."

Once again, he turned toward Manolis. "Look, grandpa, we are not stupid. We know that you have money. You have a rich son that has many rental buildings in Salonika. You have a rich American son that has just returned from overseas with lots of money and gold watches he brought from the United States. We make you an offer to protect your family from the evil bandits in this area and you ignore my request and shun me like I am some poor beggar."

"Look," stated Alexander, "I do have some money. A little. I keep it in the bank, but not in the form of cash. I can go to the bank tomorrow and get you your money. How much does my father owe you?"

"Two hundred and fifty thousand drachmas," stated Forfolias.

"No problem," said Alexander. "If you just give me some time"—he looked down at his watch—"I can be back here by noon tomorrow with your money."

Forfolias noticed the gold watch on the wrist of Alexander. He looked and he could see that Manolis had a similar watch.

"Let me have your watches as collateral," he told the men.

They both handed over their watches to Forfolias.

"Nice watches," Forfolias commented. "A gift from America?"

Alexander nodded yes as Forfolias placed one of the watches on his own wrist and tossed the second watch to Laventis.

"You know," said Forfolias, "I believe your other sons can come up with my money. Right now, I'm more interested in sending home a message that will ensure that the people of Avgerinos take me seriously from now on."

Forfolias nodded at Maras who took his signal, raised up his yataghan sword, and swung it at Alexander's head. Alexander stretched his hands outward into a defensive posture. In one swipe of his sword, Maras managed to slice through the hands of Alexander and lop off his head where he stood.

Severed fingers went flying. His body buckled at the knees and fell to the ground. His head rolled out about fifteen feet in front of his son, Plato, who just stood there in complete shock at what he just witnessed.

Immediately, Leventis struck Manolis in the lower back with a kick that knocked the wind out of him. Manolis crumbled to the ground onto his knees.

Maras and Leventis scrambled to grab the old man, seemingly ignoring Plato who stood there like a statue, afraid to move and unable to breathe. The two men dragged Manolis over to a tree and tied him up. They placed his hands behind him and wrapped them around the base of the tree. They tied him so tight that he let out a scream as one of his shoulder joints snapped and popped out of place.

Manolis could hear and feel a tearing sensation as tendons and ligaments separated while the rope was pulled tighter. Manolis sat helpless, his feet straight out in front of him as he gazed at his beheaded son and then glanced over to his beloved grandson who was simply standing there, not knowing what to do.

"Please don't hurt my grandson," begged Manolis as tears ran down his face.

"Don't worry, old man. We need someone to deliver our message and to bear witness to what happens to those who disobey us. I'm sure your grandson is a good boy and will deliver this message as we expect." Forfolias looked over at Plato.

Plato was frozen with fear. He couldn't move. What he just witnessed was more than any eleven-year-old child could bear. Earlier that day he felt like a man, but now he wished he could curl up in his mother's arms and lap to escape this nightmare.

"Today is your lucky day, boy," Maras said to Plato with a smile, as if teasing him like a little brother. Maras slapped Plato on the back as if to congratulate him.

As Jelalis observed the scene that was before him, even he was shocked at the brutality and carnage he was witnessing. He knew that they might kill Manolis and whomever he was with, but he wasn't expecting a beheading.

He looked down at the body of Alexander and then glanced at the head. He quietly wished it had been Yiannis's body and head that were lying there instead of Yiannis's innocent American brother whom Jelalis hardly knew and had not seen in over a decade.

No matter, Jelalis though. *Revenge is revenge.*

Jelalis then looked into the face of Plato. He didn't know the boy, but he could tell he was related to the Exarhopouloses. The only thought that immediately ran through his mind at that moment was that Pavlos and Yiannis would definitely come looking for him when this boy told his uncles that the man without a nose was present at the assassination of their father and brother.

"I think we should also kill the boy." Jelalis rapidly spoke up to the Albanian leader. "The village will know that I'm involved if you let him go."

"What is there to be afraid of?" said Forfolias. "You are under my protection now. We are stronger than these village peasants. You see what happens when they disobey us." He gestured at the body and head of Alexander sprawled out in the grass before them.

Jelalis repeated his objection. "This is not a good idea. We cannot have any witnesses to what happens here. It will surely put us in danger with the authorities. We need to dispatch both the old man and his grandson now!"

"Nonsense," Forfolias stated. "My decision is final."

Forfolias didn't like his decisions to be questioned. Plus, his decision was not made out of mercy. They clearly stated in their letters to the villagers and farmers that they would kill their children if their demands were not met. This decision would ensure an added element of cruelty and terror for all the villagers to see. The bandits knew word would spread throughout the region, and they could now strong-arm anyone they wanted.

"Come here, boy," said Forfolias. "I want you to take a good look and to remember what happens to those who disobey your new Uncle Forfolias."

He beckoned the boy to come closer to the tree where his grandfather was tied. Plato couldn't move, so Maras came up behind him and shoved him in the direction of Forfolias and his bound grandfather.

Manolis was screaming out of anger, fear, and the loss of his second oldest son. Forfolias grabbed the old man by his hair and pulled upward stretching out his neck and exposing his throat.

"Leventis," he said, "give me your sword."

Leventis handed Forfolias his yataghan. Rather than swinging in one stroke like Maras did with Alexander, Forfolias sawed into Manolis neck from the front of his throat and sliced clear through it to the back of his neck like carving a piece of meat.

Manolis let out a primal scream that was cut short by a gurgling sound that only an animal could make. Then, he began drowning in the blood that poured down his throat from his severed carotid arteries. The sound was sickening as the sword made its way through the vertebrae. Blood spewed everywhere. It shot up onto the clothes and faces of Forfolias and Leventis, who stood too close. It got all over the tree, and of course it started soaking into the dirt at the base of the roots.

As a sick joke, Forfolias tossed the head of Manolis at Jelalis, who wasn't expecting it. He was standing far enough away from the tree so as not to get blood all over him. Forfolias saw this and thought it funny to bring Jelalis into the mess and carnage they were creating as a group.

Jelalis didn't react quick enough to get out of the way, and now his shirt, face, and hands were splattered with blood as he batted the head down to the ground in front of him.

The Albanians laughed at Jelalis, and then began to dance among the bodies, slapping their feet into the blood-soaked dirt as they hummed, whistled, and sang a song in their native language that neither Plato nor Jelalis could understand.

Dancing around the bodies of their victims was quite common by Albanian bandits. It was almost a ritual. The same thing was recounted by a mother in the area of Plessa under circumstances that were just as savage. After slaughtering the woman's son, the bandits forced her to serve them food and pour them wine while they danced around the corpse until morning.

Jelalis was appalled by the macabre scene before him. He had committed robberies and burglaries with them. He had extorted bribes with them. But never before had he committed or witnessed such a brutal act of killing. Although he was satisfied to have exacted his own revenge on the family, he was equally ill at ease at the fact that none of the bodies lying before him were that of Yiannis. He wanted Yiannis dead more than any other Exarhopoulos.

He quickly thought of a way he could also lure Yiannis into this trap without him knowing it was he that set the family up. His mind also raced to come up with a plan to kill this young witness before he got back to Avgerinos with his story of the man with no nose. He had no quick solutions. He was stuck.

"Boy," Forfolias shouted at Plato. "Start loading up the bodies!"

CHAPTER 11

Silent Dirges

Plato started with the body of his father. He briefly clung to the absurd notion that if he could go to him, comfort him, check on him, perhaps his father would not really be dead. He went over to the body, and of course it was completely lifeless.

At first, he attempted to grasp the wrists of his father's corpse in order to drag the body closer to the cart. However, he simply wasn't strong enough and his grip slipped over his father's hands. Plato fell back onto his rump.

He then decided he didn't want to drag the body in that manner anyway because his view was straight down the open, gaping wound of his father's neck where his head should have been.

He moved around toward the legs of his father's corpse. This time he tried gripping both ankles, one in each hand. Again, his grip wasn't strong enough for him to hold on. He then tried using both hands on one ankle. This method allowed him to make some progress.

The entire time he wrestled with maneuvering his father's body toward the cart, he struggled to stay calm. He was keenly aware the Albanians could change their minds and kill him at any moment. The panic was inescapable.

He continued moving the body, yard by yard. He pulled, dragged, stopped to rest, re-gripped, and started the process all over again. The distance to the cart was only about twenty-five yards, but by the time he reached it, he was completely drenched in sweat. The heat of the day was oppressive as it neared noon, and he didn't dare ask for a drink of water.

Once he got the body to the back of the cart, the next task was to get it *into* the cart. If he was barely strong enough to drag the body twenty-five yards, how on earth, he wondered, was he going to get the lifeless body of his father up onto the back floorboards?

First, he tried picking up the corpse by hugging it as he hugged his father so many times before. This was unbearable, though, because his face was now right at the opening where his dad's head used to be. He could see inside. He could see the chords and vessels and parts of the throat and neck that he couldn't identify. It was too much for him. He couldn't do it physically, and he couldn't do it mentally. He let the body drop out of exhaustion after his first attempt. When it fell, more blood spattered from the open cavity and onto the dirt of the trail.

Leventis laughed when the body hit the ground. Forfolias, Maras, and Jelalis lit cigarettes and were just chatting to themselves, watching this helpless eleven-year-old boy struggle with the bodies of his relatives. Leventis reached into a bag that he had been carrying and brought out a bottle of cognac. The men drank, smoked, and talked as if having a picnic on holiday.

Plato stood there for a moment. This had to be done. He would not allow himself to fail, for failure meant possible death for himself. He needed to comply with the bandits' orders. He didn't want to risk angering the Albanians. He looked into the cart and saw a fairly lengthy piece of rope. Then, he got an idea.

He took the rope and tied it to one of his father's ankles. He then got into the cart and hoisted the leg up to the edge of the platform by pulling upwards on the rope as far as he could. Keeping the rope taut and his father's leg suspended, he then looped the rope around a hook toward the front of the cart and tied it off to one of the boards.

Plato jumped down and got into a squat position under the body. Cupping the body with his arms, he stood up and lifted the body up onto the cart, rolling it onto the back end of the wooden platform. In the process of performing this act of lifting, blood poured out of the open cavity all over Plato's hands, arms, shirt, and pants. It dripped down onto his shoes. He was now covered in his father's blood.

Pushing the body forward, he slid it a little further so it would not fall out, then hopped onto the cart and dragged the body toward the front. He untied the ankle. He would need to repeat this process again for his grandfather's body. All the while, he fought back his terror and the urge to cry. He couldn't show weakness. Not now.

The body of his grandfather had to be untied from the tree before it could be moved. When he tried untying the entire mess of rope, it was so tight that the knots simply refused to budge. He went to the cart and retrieved a small axe he remembered seeing there on the ride to Tsativi.

For a moment, the Albanians' guard went up when they saw Plato holding a weapon in his hands. But they shrugged it off, knowing that the small boy was in no condition to put up a fight or mount an attack.

Plato hacked at the ropes about a dozen times before it came loose. Manolis's body first slumped forward and then to the side before it fell to the ground in a prone position. Blood came pouring out of the open cavity at the neck and spattered onto the dirt, leaves, roots, and grass around the tall tree.

Plato repeated the entire process with his grandfather's body. While hoisting the body of this grandfather onto the cart, he began thinking about his next task. He still had to retrieve the heads. He didn't want to. He didn't want to touch them.

Just as he was finishing pulling his grandfather's body closer to the middle of the cart next to the body of his father, Forfolias who was by now losing his patience with Plato's slow pace, walked over to the heads. He picked them both up by the hair in each hand and tossed them into the cart on top of the bodies.

Plato was repulsed by Forfolias's callousness, although by now it should not have come as a surprise to him. He was exhausted and emotionally numb. He leaned over the cart and vomited. Gasping for breath between his loud, violent heaving, he could hear a couple of the Albanians laughing.

When he was finished his regurgitation, the Albanian gang leader walked up to him.

"Hurry home now, boy. Tell the people of Avgerinos that this is what happens when they don't pay their taxes. We will be back in three days to collect on the promise your American father made to us. Don't look back."

Forfolias had nothing to worry about concerning Plato's gaze. Plato couldn't get out of there fast enough. He clicked the reigns and the donkeys complied. They headed up the trail toward Avgerinos and away from the murder scene.

Another compelling reason that kept Plato's eyes fixated ahead of him was because he didn't want to see the corpses of his relatives bouncing and rolling around in the back of the cart. With every stone and rut the wagon wheels rolled over, the bodies shimmied and the heads partially rolled side to side.

The back of the cart pooled with blood by now and was dripping over and through the floorboards onto the trail below. But the flow of fluid only lasted a short while as it started to coagulate while rigor mortis set in.

An hour into the ride already seemed an eternity. Plato was thirsty, exhausted, sweaty, dirty, and bloody. He was in shock from the trauma of what he had experienced, and he felt as if he was separated from his own body. He could almost see himself driving the cart. It was as if he was watching himself in a dream from above. However, this was no dream. It was a living nightmare that was going to last a very long time.

Just then, he looked up ahead of him and could see Thomas rounding the top of the hill toward him. Thomas was slow-jogging with a sack of what was to be their lunch slumped over his shoulder and held by a cord. Thomas was immediately perplexed as to why the cart was making its way back toward him so soon. As he got closer to the cart, it became even more perplexing as to why Plato was driving it and the men were nowhere to be seen. Had there been an accident?

Plato stopped the cart right in front of Thomas. Thomas could see that the boy had a look of horror on his face and was covered in sweat and blood. Thomas's eyes flung open, and he demanded what was going on. Plato said nothing. He just stared at Thomas as if looking *through* him.

Thomas asked again, but a little more gently now, "Plato, where are your father and grandfather?"

Plato turned his head slightly as if to point with his eyes toward the back of the cart. He then looked straight through Thomas again. Thomas walked around to the back of the cart. When he looked in, he yelled out a curse that Plato had never heard before.

Thomas panicked and became frantic. He started firing a barrage of questions at Plato. "Who did this? What happened? Where are they now?"

Plato simply replied, "Bandits told me to bring the bodies back to the village as a warning. They said they wanted money. I couldn't stop them. I couldn't stop them!"

It was then he broke down and started crying. He fell down onto to the floorboards of the cart's front seat.

Thomas climbed up and took the reins. He looked around as he hurried the donkeys along and headed back toward Avgerinos. His main concern at the moment was getting back to the village in one piece and in ensuring the safety of the Exarhopoulos boy. There was no telling if the people who did this to his boss and his boss' son were following or in the process of surrounding them in an attempted ambush. Plato lay on the floor next to Thomas's feet and sobbed uncontrollably.

As they got closer to the village and could finally make out the cemetery at the top of the hill, Thomas started to think about what on earth he was going to say when they entered the village. What would he tell the family? How were Plato's siblings going to react? What was he to tell Plato's poor mother, Kalliope? She was about to lose her entire world.

His thoughts went to the preservation of the surviving family members' feelings. He then thought about Plato and what he had witnessed. In the past two and a half hours, Plato must have aged thirty years. Thomas began to assign guilt to himself for not being there to protect his boss and his boss's family.

When they finally entered the village, there didn't seem to be anyone around. It was still early in the afternoon, just past 2:00 p.m. The men were surely out tending crops and driving sheep. The women were probably just getting started with preparing the evening meals for their families. It was hot, so the children were playing someplace indoors. One of the village women looked out the window of her home and saw Thomas driving the cart by himself.

"Thomas," she called out to him. "Where is Manolis and Alexander? Didn't you just leave here a while ago with food for them?"

Thomas said nothing. Plato, exhausted from having poured all of his emotions out over the past hour's drive, peeked his head up from the floorboards of the cart and just stared at the woman through the window with an expressionless look on his face.

It was then that the woman noticed Plato slumped down on the floor of the front seat of the cart. Even from the distant window, she could sense something was terribly wrong. She glanced toward the back of the cart as it passed under her window, and she could now see both of the bodies. Her eyes flew wide open and she ran outside to Plato and Thomas.

Shock overtook the woman as she approached the cart and looked in to confirm what she saw from her bedroom window. She saw the bodies and the heads tossed about in the cart. Blood was caked everywhere, much of it soaked into the floorboards and the hay. She let out a scream. Everyone in the village could hear it.

Those villagers in earshot stopped what they were doing and looked in the direction the scream came from. Children stopped playing and stepped out of their homes onto front stoops. Everyone was listening for another scream or noise that would indicate what the matter was or to confirm what they had heard to be a cry of shock. That's when it started. Violent crying and screaming continued as soon as the woman caught her breath from her initial scream. The villagers came running.

From the nearby fields, the men who could hear the commotion stopped their work and ran toward the village. Word spread quickly through the fields that something was wrong. They ran back into Avgerinos, ready to tackle whatever problem they had to face and to help whomever was in need.

Pavlos and Yiannis pushed their way past the villagers who now surrounded the cart. Many of them were sobbing. Some of them were yelling and demanding to know what had happened. All of them were in a state of disbelief.

When they looked down at the headless corpses of their relatives, Pavlos and Yiannis also began to scream in anger and sorrow. The screaming grew to a frenzy when their mother gazed down upon the bodies of her husband, Manolis and her American son. Shouts of the villagers with questions came in rapid succession toward Thomas and Plato who just sat there, silent and motionless in the driver's seat of the cart. Plato looked down at the blood on his pant legs and shoes. He didn't say a word. He couldn't.

Thomas hopped off the cart and pulled Pavlos and Yiannis to the side and told him what little he knew of what happened. He told them how he came back to the village to retrieve forgotten water and food for their father, brother, and nephew and how, while jogging back to the men, he came upon Plato and the cart. He told them that the only thing Plato said was that bandits had killed them and made Plato bring the bodies back as a warning to the village.

Kalliope and her three other children were some of the last on the scene because their home was built close to the top of the hill. It was one of the farthest distances to traverse to the edge of the village where Thomas had stopped the cart. As she approached, she saw Plato still mounted on the cart. She knew something terrible had happened. Her premonition was coming true.

Yiannis stopped Kalliope before she could get close enough to see the body of her husband. She started screaming and crying and insisted she go to her husband. Yiannis tried telling her that he had been killed and that she should not see what was in the cart. She insisted with her screams. She flailed her arms as she fought and clawed and kicked to get closer to her husband. When she gazed upon the corpses and the heads, she immediately recognized the head of her beloved husband of over a dozen years. She gasped, then fainted right there onto the cobblestone street.

Plato's oldest uncle, Kostas, reached for the boy with outstretched arms. Plato went to his uncle, hugging him tight as Kostas helped him off the cart. He held the boy in his arms in a strong embrace and walked away from the scene of people screaming, crying, and debating as to what to do now.

Plato hung on for dear life, searching for security and sanctuary from the violence and danger he had witnessed only hours before. There would never be enough comfort in the embrace to remotely wash away the pain he felt and the horror now etched in his memory forever. He couldn't even turn to his mother right now, as he watched the family carry her unconscious body back up the streets toward their home.

Spiliotis, the village station chief of police, beckoned for Kostas to bring Plato to the police station for questioning. Spiliotis wanted to get the interrogations over with quickly so he could gather a posse and go after whoever did this. Kostas sat Plato down on a bench within the office. He brought him a cup of water and urged Plato to take a drink. Plato was so thirsty. He hadn't had any water since they left for the fields of Tsativi early that morning.

As Plato gulped huge mouthfuls of water, Kostas took a damp rag and tried to wash some of the dried blood off of the boy's face and hands.

"Are you hurt?" asked Spiliotis. "Did they injure you in any way?"

Plato shook his head no.

Meanwhile, a discussion broke out in the center square as to what to do with the bodies. They wanted to take the bodies immediately to the church for burial rights, but the superstitious priests vehemently objected. They told the family they could not bring the bodies into their homes, nor could they bring them into the church for burial preparations due to the fact that the bodies were dismembered. Anger broke out among the family members.

"How can we ensure our men get a proper Christian burial?" one of them shouted.

Nothing could be done. They couldn't go against the mandate of the church. The villagers left the bodies in the cart and small coffins were quickly assembled. The bodies were placed inside and were carried to the top of the hill to the cemetery and buried in the Exarhopoulos family plot. The Forfolias gang had obviously foreseen this. They had to have known the bodies would receive no proper rights. It made the killings even that much more painful for the family.

After placing the bodies of their brother and father in their family plot, Pavlos and Yiannis walked over to the police station. They were anxious to speak with Plato and Thomas. They needed to know what happened. Their shock and feelings of loss quickly turned into anger for the perpetrators of this crime.

Plato couldn't speak at first. The men were very gentle in their questioning and told him to take his time. Plato told them of the bandits, how they asked for money.

"The Bandits said they gave Papou Manolis a letter that he did not heed," Plato recalled.

He then told them how many bandits were in the group. When Spiliotis asked Plato for descriptions, the one description that stood out was the man with no nose.

Plato went on with recounting the murders and how they seemed to happen with no warning. The outright cruelty of what they did and how they made this poor boy witness these murders was atrocious beyond anything the three brothers and the police chief could think of. Their anger grew.

Pavlos told his brothers to stay with the boy for a moment. He ran back to his home and rifled through his father's paperwork. It didn't take long to find the letter the Albanians sent him.

Why didn't father tell us of these threats? Pavlos thought. *Yiannis and I are more than capable of fighting back against these thugs. After all, there were only four bandits.*

Both Pavlos and Yiannis spent time in the military and Yiannis already had proven himself in his altercation with Jelalis five years prior. There was no reason to hide this from the family. Then it dawned on him. His father was probably concealing this threat from their brother, Alexander. Their father most likely didn't want to alarm his American son and his family. He wanted them to feel comfortable coming back from America.

Pavlos raced back to the station and presented the chief with the letter. The anger all of the men felt was just too much. They would have their revenge upon these Albanian dogs and they would finally put an end to Jelalis's treachery too.

Spiliotis sent word to his superiors about the murder. Fortunately, a man who was quickly becoming renown in Macedonia as a killer of bandits was already in the area. Sergeant Markos Trimpos arrived on the scene the following morning while Papaconstantinou was gathering his men and forming a posse with anyone in the village who wanted to participate.

"I'll take over from here," said Trimpos.

Papaconstantinou was only all too happy to hand over the authority to Markos Trimpos. It was an honor to finally meet the man who was gaining such a strong reputation in the military for bringing Albanian criminals to justice. Everyone in the village was in awe of this man as he stood in the square and began to give instructions on how they would proceed in capturing the Forfolias gang, once and for all.

Pavlos and Yiannis instantly fell in step. Their time in the military was not so distant in their past and they relished the thought of joining in with Trimpos to bring their family members' murderers to justice.

CHAPTER 12

Markos Trimpos

Two years before the Exarhopoulos murders, Markos Trimpos found himself standing on the edge of an olive tree orchard over a pool of blood. He was finishing his task of packing the head of Gregory Zafeiroulis in a sack after wrapping it in cheese cloth and salt. It would be displayed in the center of Lefkada for all to see as a warning to bandits never to prey upon the community again. Zafeiroulis had terrorized the island of Lefkada for over eighteen years with his gang of thieves and murderers. They stole livestock, extorted money, and killed anyone who so much as voiced an objection or resisted.

The authorities spent nearly two decades trying to bring Zafeiroulis to justice. In the process, he and his gang killed over fourteen soldiers and four sergeants. He was truly one of the most feared and wanted men in all of Greece.

Markos Trimpos received his orders to hunt down Zafeiroulis just days after being promoted to staff sergeant. He was a rising star in the gendarmes and was rapidly making a name for himself as the ultimate bandit killer. He was also quickly moving up in rank with each successful mission.

Trimpos stood five feet, ten inches tall. He had a barrel chest, a large head with full, thick black hair and a neck that was nearly the width of his head. He wore a thick black mustache and had the build of someone who might have been into resistance weight training. His wrists were as thick as his muscular forearms, and he was known for his extraordinarily strong grip.

He built his physique chopping and dragging wood with his father as a young teenager in his home village. They sold the split wood to the villagers to supplement the family's livelihood. Markos would have continued in the family business after his brief, obligatory stint in the military. However, he found he had a penchant for military life and decided to make a career of it.

When he showed up for military duty in the spring of 1924, he immediately made a positive impression on his peers and superiors. Trimpos was more physically adept than most men, could easily negotiate the training obstacles and was a quick study of military tactics. He was also one of the best marksmen in the unit.

He earned the respect of his peers for being a man of integrity who went "by the book." Rarely did he touch alcohol and was a stickler for military discipline. He relished in the honor and fidelity that was instilled in him through military protocol.

One week after he finished basic training, his unit was given orders to track down an Albanian bandit by the name of Andraes Stavrou who was wanted in Kleisouri. Markos picked him off with a single shot of his open-sighted rifle as Andraes fled from a stable he had been hiding in and ran across an open field. They estimated the distance to be more than four hundred yards.

Just one month later he proved that he wasn't just going to be a killer of bandits but would also take them into custody. When his unit surrounded three bandits led by Alexandros Hodos in a village hamlet on the outskirts of Konitsa, Trimpos engaged in negotiations during a standoff that lasted over twelve hours. Markos Trimpos negotiated a surrender agreement and managed to convince the bandits to give up under promises of leniency and a fair trial.

Just two weeks later, he and his unit managed to capture alive two more Albanian bandits who were sent to an Ioannina court and sentenced to death for their string of murders.

And now, after a three-hour battle with Gregory Zafeiroulis, he had his head neatly packed in a burlap sack, ready to be transported to the governor of Lefkada where they would display the head in the middle of the town square for all to see. This string of four successful missions would elevate him to a sergeant's position. Soon he would be rewarded with complete command over a detachment in charge of the entire region of Epirus.

After the killing of Zafeiroulis, he turned his attention north-ward, leaving Lefkada a much safer community. He received notice from his superiors about a bandit gang led by two Albanians by the name of Tsiogas and Tsaimos. Typical of Albanian bandits, both men worked in unison as they robbed cheese traders, stole sheep, and took villagers as hostages for reward money.

Trimpos caught up with them in August of 1926 and cornered the men in a villager's house they had broken into. After a brief gun battle, Tsiogas lay dead on the floor of the home with a gunshot wound to his head, and Tsaimos lay injured in the master bedroom corner, holding onto his shoulder where he had been shot through from front to back. They bandaged up Tsaimos and delivered him to the authorities where he was sentenced to death and executed by firing squad a few months later.

After this successful campaign, Sergeant Markos Trimpos received orders to eradicate one of the most dangerous and notorious Albanian gangs in all of Macedonia. The name of the gang: Forfolias.

CHAPTER 13

Evasion and Justice

After committing a murder, Christos Forfolias liked to move from the area quickly to avoid discovery by the authorities and to elude vengeful family members. He looked down upon the people he terrorized and viewed them as simple village farmers or peasants. He knew the symbolic message he sent back with the young Greek boy would have the desired impact. He was confident it would make the people in the area submissive to his future demands. However, he also knew patrols of police and vigilantes were in constant search of bandit gangs like his throughout the area. Therefore, he took no chances.

Forfolias moved the gang south and into the village of Pentalafos to wait out the search parties that would surely be looking for them.

"We'll wait here for a few days," Forfolias told the men as they entered the village square. "Later we'll send word to the villagers of Avgerinos of our demands. I think we will ask for 500,000 drachmas now."

They went directly to the home of a local fruit vendor by the name of Michalis, a Pentalafos resident who had given them shelter in the past. Michalis previously proved to be quite useful to Forfolias in providing the gang with information and gossip regarding posse movements and targets of opportunity. He also sheltered and fed the gang when they were on the run. He was paid well for his efforts, and the gang knew they could trust him.

After a few nights of rest, Forfolias sent Michalis into the landscape between Avgerinos and Pentalafos to seek out a shepherd to convey his message. When Michalis returned just two hours later, Forfolias was surprised.

"It only took you two hours to find someone?" Forfolias asked Michalis.

"Boss," said Michalis with a worried look on his face, "there is a group of men just on the outskirts of the village who are heading right toward us. I ran back as fast as I could. You need to clear out of here."

"I told you the Exarhopoulos brothers would not simply let the death of their father and brother go," chided Jelalis.

He had been nagging Forfolias for letting the son of Alexander go free. He was becoming quite an annoyance to Forfolias after several times repeating his opinion that it was a terrible mistake. Now, with a posse closing in on their position, it seemed Forfolias was finally realizing how right Jelalis was.

"Well, my friends," Forfolias addressed his gang. "Perhaps we should abandon our hopes for Exarhopoulos money and retire back to Albania. I think we've made enough in the Macedonian mountains."

And with that statement, they were off to the border of Greece and Albania.

They moved through the back streets of Pentalafos, keeping their heads down so as not to draw attention by the neighbors or to be recognized. Forfolias's new plan was to simply slip across the border into Albania without alerting the authorities. They would be safe there from reprisals. The gang had accumulated a little over two million drachmas from their collected bribes and robberies. It was time to go home.

The day before the posse closed in on the gang near Pentalafos, George Konas was taken into custody by the Avgerinos police chief, Spiliotis, and escorted to Kozani for questioning. Konas confessed that he, in fact, harbored the Forfolias gang several times during their excursions.

"They told me they would kill me if I didn't put them up in my cabin," he stated.

He was adamant that he never participated in any of the murders. He also gave a strange account of the murders of Alexander and Manolis Exarhopoulos that was posted in the papers on October 9. His statement described the murders as having taken place in his cabin, and he recounted a dialogue between perpetrator and victim which included a last will and testament that Forfolias made Manolis write before severing his head.

The authorities didn't believe his account. Too many aspects of Konas's story didn't add up. Plus, they knew the murders took place in Tsativi from Plato's account and the obvious evidence they found at the murder scene. It was obvious Konas wasn't even a witness to the murders since he never even mentioned the young boy being present.

The prosecutor decided that Konas was trying to get in on the reward money. Having nothing to hold him on, they dropped all charges and sent him on his way.

Konas never collected any reward money. He went back to herding sheep and never again spoke about the murders or his part in harboring the Forfolias gang.

While the authorities were releasing Konas, Pavlos, Yiannis, and the posse they were now attached to were closing in on Pentalafos. Unfortunately, the gang managed to exit the village less than an hour before the posse arrived.

The men of Avgerinos frantically questioned everyone they could find. Someone had to have information or at least had seen the gang as they passed through the area. They mentioned the reward money in case that might entice someone to speak up.

It worked. Michalis confessed that the gang spent a few nights at his home. He told them that he was terrified of Forfolias and that he was made to harbor the gang or else be killed.

"How long ago did they leave?" Trimpos asked

"About an hour ago. You just missed them," stated Michalis.

Michalis calculated that the posse was so close, Forfolias would sure to be captured or killed. He told them the gang headed due west toward the border.

Meanwhile, Forfolias and his gang were beating feet to gain some ground between them and their predators.

"When we reach Anaselitsa, we'll stop for the night and rest there," Forfolias said. "We'll push ourselves hard today. No stopping until then!"

It was a ballsy move. Anaselitsa was the village where they murdered the shepherd just prior to the Exarhopoulos murders. Laventis protested and thought they may get caught there by vigilante family members of the shepherd.

"No," Forfolias insisted. "It is our best option to stop and rest for a while. We can always hide out in an outlaying farmhouse instead of entering the town. This way, we will draw much less attention to ourselves."

They were exhausted by the time they reached Anaselitsa. They hadn't eaten all day, drank little water, and were covered from head to toe in dirt and sweat. The bandits forced their way into a farmer's home and made the family feed and bed them for the evening.

Up to this point, Jelalis was still tagging along with the Forfolias gang. However, by the time they reached Anaselitsa, Forfolias decided there was no more use for the man with no nose.

Forfolias turned to Jelalis as they lay on their bedding, trying to drift off to sleep.

"Tomorrow we must split up. You cannot come to the border with us."

Jelalis was shocked.

"Why do we need to part company? I've been loyal to you and I want to come with you to Albania. I'm a dead man if I stay here in the mountains. You made sure of that when you let that American boy go free. He will identify me and they all know who I am."

"Which is exactly why we must split up now. Entering any village before we cross the border will bring attention to our movements. You must hide out in the mountains and avoid capture. You can do that alone. You will give us all away as soon as anyone sees you."

Forfolias continued his attempt to reason with Jelalis. "Hide out in the mountains for a month or so, then come across the border later and meet up with us. We will have a home for you there."

It was a lie. Both men knew it but neither would admit it. The fact was Forfolias could care less what happened to Jelalis. He was becoming a liability. They could no longer enter a village and disguise their own identity if they had a man with a hole in his face among their entourage. It wasn't something they could easily conceal.

Jelalis continued his protest. "I can help you through the mountains better than anyone. We don't even need to enter any villages. Who knows the land better than I?"

"Laventis, Maras, and I already know the mountains well enough, my friend," replied Forfolias. "You forget we've spent years here among you Greeks."

The plea was fruitless. Jelalis was rejected and abandoned in a field along the outskirts of Anaselitsa. No one knew him there, and no one wanted to. Forfolias was right. Word had already spread quickly of the man with no nose and the posse now turned its attention due west.

"I don't care if those dogs make it all the way to Albania," Yiannis told Pavlos. "I say we follow them across the border if we don't get to them beforehand."

Pavlos agreed, but the brothers decided to keep their intentions a secret from the other men in the posse. They knew crossing the border would not be an option for the lawmen. If it came to that, though, they'd have to go it alone.

They tracked the bandits for over two weeks, following them into the mountains of Avdela in Grevena, into the mountains of Ipirus, and eventually into the forested regions just outside of Konitsa.

Forfolias, Maras, and Laventis managed to gain some distance between them and the posse but were never able to get more than three hours ahead of their pursuers.

"We'll take no chances tonight," Forfolias said on the last evening before they were to cross the border. "We will make camp in the forest and leave the villagers alone so as not to alert anyone of our presence. We will wait a while after the sun goes down, then leave in the cover of darkness and move in the middle of the night. Before daylight, we'll break for the border."

Forfolias felt they could easily slip across the border undetected and be free to retire off the fruits of their bounty. As fortune would have it, the gang came across a shepherd's cabin in the woods. They would have a roof over their heads before their last push home.

On September 23, while preparing a meal for breakfast over a fire, Markos Trimpos received reliable information from a local farmer that the Forfolias gang was staying in a shepherd's quarters in the mountain village outskirts of Lioupsako.

"By my calculations," Markos told the rest of the posse, "the gang will most likely head in a northward direction toward the border. My guess is they will do this at night time. We must move fast."

Pavlos and Yiannis glanced at each other. Finally, they had a chance at bringing their relatives' killers to justice.

Trimpos set up an ambush deep within a ravine in a wooded area called Tsoupotiri. He calculated the Forfolias gang would be sure to approach from the northeastern fields and into the wood line, where they would lay in wait. The trail that cut through the ravine was faint, but was the only conceivable path for crossing the border unless the bandits wanted to hack their way through the brush and sticker bushes. Trimpos was confident that the gang would surely have to pass this way.

"If we can take them alive," Trimpos told the men, "then let's do that. However, take no chances. If we must kill them, then so be it."

He gave orders to the posse to wait for his command, then shoot to kill.

It was 9:00 p.m. when the posse set up their ambush and settled into their positions. Everyone's hearts were beating fast from the adrenaline coursing through their bodies. The men were exhausted from their race to get ahead of the gang. They had no idea how long they would have to wait. The thought also crossed their minds that they may have already missed the gang and were too late to head them off. However, nobody spoke of it. They trusted Markos Trimpos's instincts and calculations that the gang would soon traverse the path they now pointed rifles toward.

Two hours into their wait and the men were fighting their urge to fall asleep. The adrenaline dump had passed, and it caused each man to grow weary.

Pavlos and Yiannis were antsy and fought the urge to get up and go look for the gang through the forest. However, they held their ground and sat like statues in the positions Trimpos placed them in.

The posse set up in a triangular pattern that could cover the entire ravine without shooting at their own party. The skies were clear and the night was lit by a waxing moon. With adjusted eyesight, it was not difficult to see the gang of three men approaching their position from a distance of about a hundred yards.

All of the posse could clearly see the three men and each of them wondered to themselves where the fourth man might be. There was no time to think about it now. Clearing their mind, they honed in on their targets.

Trimpos waited until the men were inside the triangle of death before he yelled, "Fire!"

Shots rang out and pierced the silence of the night. Forfolias's men were startled and stunned as some bullets whizzed by their heads while others found soft targets and pierced abdomens, legs, and arms.

Maras ran to the edge of the ravine, but unfortunately for him he ran directly at Markos Trimpos, who shot him point blank in the chest, dropping him in his tracks at Trimpos's feet.

The startled and wounded half brothers took up positions behind tree stumps. Forfolias fired back at the dark without acquiring a target. Leventis hunkered down behind a log with his sword. He felt helpless, and he was.

In their confusion, Forfolias and Laventis couldn't see that they had been facing the wrong direction. Laventis had no idea that Pavlos was directly behind him. Pavlos took careful aim and shot him in the back of the head as he lay there behind a rotten log.

Forfolias would not have as quick a death. He took two rounds, one in his arm and one in his leg. He lay bleeding in the leaves, screaming obscenities at the posse.

"You have one chance to give up and be taken alive!" Trimpos shouted.

"The hell with you!" replied Forfolias. "I will never give up!"

Everyone in the posse slowly walked up to the man, their guns pointed directly at this bandit who caused so much anguish in the region. Three of the posse shot almost at the same time and put Forfolias out of his misery.

Markos and his men then severed all three of the bandits' heads and packed them in sacks with salt to keep them preserved for display. They tossed the bodies into a shallow, natural depression in the earth and kicked leaves and dirt over them.

Pavlos spit onto the shallow grave. "No Christian burial for you, either," he stated.

In the morning, the posse began their long trek back home. They stopped near the outskirts of Lioupsako village to post the heads of Forfolias, Laventis, and Maras up on stakes. The heads were displayed there for three days. Thereafter, the heads were moved to the outskirts of Konitsa for display for another three days, and then finally brought to Ioannina, where they were displayed until the heads decomposed and fell to the earth as rotted skulls.

The gruesome warning of the Macedonians was a clear message to any future bandits who sought to return and wreak havoc on their communities. It simply would not be tolerated.

The amount of money recovered by the posse did, indeed, total close to two million drachmas. Each man in the posse was also offered reward money for their work. However, they unanimously agreed to donate all of the stolen money and reward money back to the villages and farmers that were victimized by the Forfolias gang.

There was just one question that nagged at the men in the posse: What about the man with no nose? What became of Jelalis?

"We'll put a warrant out for his arrest," Markos told the posse. "I'm sure he'll turn up somewhere. You can't hide for long when you have a hole in your head."

The posse broke out in laughter at Trimpos's joke.

Pavlos and Yiannis couldn't find anything to laugh about.

CHAPTER 14

Hostage

Jelalis found himself alone once more. He was at a loss as what to do with himself now. He liked the bandit life and felt accepted and protected by the many gangs with which he spent the last five years. He liked his "usefulness" as a thug and his ability to strike fear into various victims with his appearance. It had become an asset for this way of life. But now it was a huge burden.

Again, he cursed Forfolias for allowing the boy, Plato, to live. His only hope now was to attach himself to another gang.

Of course he had no idea that, at that very moment, the Forfolias gang was being decapitated and buried in shallow graves. He assumed they were probably across the border by now. Had he known that their heads were being displayed on stakes, he probably would have counted his blessings for having been abandoned by the gang.

He made his way into the small village of Drosopigi and sought to hide out for a few days until his pursuers got tired of looking for him and gave up.

He made his way into the village from one of the side streets where there was little foot traffic. It was just past noon and it was already very hot. He knew he would need money sooner or later. The amount Forfolias gave him as severance pay for his loyalty as they parted ways was reasonable, but it wouldn't last him more than a few weeks. He would also need food soon and a donkey or horse would go a long way in helping him survive alone for a while before he could seek out another gang to hook up with.

Maybe I'll create my own gang, he thought.

Smoke billowed from the chimney of the third house he came to. Someone was sure to be cooking inside the home. He was hungry and tired. He knocked lightly on the door, and a little girl answered. She couldn't have been more than six or seven. Her eyes flung wide open at the sight of the man with a hole in his face. Her jaw dropped and she gasped.

Jelalis smiled, then pulled a knife and forced his way inside. He wrapped his arm around the little girl and placed his knife against her throat. He then ordered the parents not to make a move. He looked around the room and saw no one else. This was just a young family getting started in life.

The girl's mother began to cry.

"Please don't hurt my only child. I beg of you! We will give you whatever you want."

"I'm not here to kill anyone," Jelalis assured her. "So long as you listen to my directions, no one will get hurt and I will be on my way."

Jelalis sat down on a chair at the kitchen table. He lifted the hysterically crying girl onto his lap.

"There now," he feigned consolation. "No need to cry. No one is going to hurt you. See?"

He placed the knife down on the table in front of him so it was no longer at the little girl's throat, but still in easy reach should the father of the girl get any ideas to attack him.

He ordered the father to come sit down across the table from him.

"I want you to leave the house and tell no one of my presence. Gather food in this bag."

He tossed his sack across the table at the man.

"Get as much money as you can muster. I also want a horse or donkey. Now do it quickly and alert no one."

"I am just a farmhand," the man protested. "I have very little money and I definitely do not have a horse."

"Being a farmhand, you should have easy access to food and a horse! I don't care how you do it. You will do this for your wife and child, no?"

The young father nodded.

"How will I know you will not harm my family while I am gone on your errand?"

He didn't want to leave his wife and young child in the hands of this horrific-looking scum for one second, and he certainly wasn't comfortable with the thought of stealing anything from his neighbors, many of which were his own relatives. However, there was nothing he could do. The man with the knife was holding all the cards. He was also holding his daughter in his lap.

"Hurry along, now," Jelalis said. "It has been a long time since I've been with a woman, and an even longer time since I've had the pleasure of a young girl. I might get busy in here if you don't get busy out there."

It was a threat that made the father's heart sink. Panic overtook him as he stepped outside and closed the door behind him.

Jelalis then turned to the young mother.

"You were making something to eat?"

The little girl finally began to calm down a bit and was no longer in hysterics. She just whimpered, shaking in the hideously disfigured man's arms.

"I'm hungry. I'll take some."

"Our lunch is almost done," said the woman. "I just need a few more minutes to finish preparations."

She got up from the table and went over to the stove.

"I'm in no hurry," said Jelalis. "It has been weeks since I've had a good home-cooked meal. I can be patient a bit longer. By the smell of your cooking, I can tell you must be a very good cook."

She didn't respond to the compliment.

The young mother reached into the cupboard for the spices she needed to put the finishing touches on the avgolemono soup she was preparing. When the cupboard doors came open, her eyes immediately honed in on a bottle of arsenic that the family sometimes used for medicinal purposes. This was to be her salvation, she thought. Could it be this easy?

She brought out three bowls and poured soup into each of them. Her hands were shaking as she poured a thimbleful of arsenic into the soup that was meant for Jelalis. Her heart and mind raced. It was a huge risk. What if this didn't work? What if it only made him sick? What if it didn't immediately kill him? If he didn't immediately die, would it only enrage the man? Was she putting herself and her daughter in even greater danger?

She placed his bowl in front of him first, then another to the side of her daughter as if to make the gesture they would all eat together. She sat down across the table from the bandit and placed her own bowl in front of her.

Jelalis sipped at the soup. He then asked if the woman had any cognac. "No, but I can get you some water," she replied.

"I should have told your husband to bring me cognac. Who on earth doesn't have cognac in their home for guests?" Jelalis asked sarcastically, almost angrily.

Ignoring his criticism, she poured him a cup of water to help wash down the lunch she specially prepared for him.

Within minutes, Jelalis began violently choking and coughing. The girl jumped down off his lap and ran over to her mother who held her arms wide open for her. Mom and daughter backed up into the corner of the room, her arms around her young daughter and her hands over the little girl's eyes as if to protect her from what was about to happen in their family kitchen.

Jelalis stood up from the table, knocking over the chair behind him and holding his throat. He was foaming at the mouth. The woman watched him writhe in pain and fight for air. He then fell face-first onto the table and slid off onto the floor, convulsing and choking. It took less than a minute for the disfigured man to expire.

CHAPTER 15

Returning

Kalliope never wanted to come back to Greece in the first place. She had premonitions and dreams that something bad would happen. And now her premonition had become her reality. No matter how hard her in-laws pleaded and tried to reason with her, she wanted to go home. She insisted she would return to the United States with her children.

The problem now facing her was tenfold. She had no husband to return with her. The family lost their main source of income. She had four mouths to feed and this was compounded by the collapse of the US stock market, which now brought on the Great Depression. In addition, it would be months before she could get a passport and a sponsor to attain passage back to America and her home in Marlborough, MA.

The entire community of Avgerinos struggled to find a way they could help this grieving widow and her four young children. The stress was only magnified by their own grief for the loss of their patriarch and their favorite "American" cousin. Everyone in the village was mourning the tragedy in their own way.

Kalliope still had access to their family savings account from the sale of their home in the States and whatever they saved to come to Greece. However, with inflation and the Great Depression upon them, it wouldn't go nearly as far as they had originally planned.

Alexander's family knew it would take a while for Kalliope to get her immigration paperwork and plans in order, so that gave them plenty of time to save the money to pay for passage back to the United States and to resettle in their hometown of Marlborough.

Her brother in law Kostas recommended to leave her oldest son, Plato with him when she was to return to the United States. Kostas promised to care for the boy in his home in Salonika and to provide Plato with the best education money could buy. Upon graduation he agreed to send Plato to America to live with the family, where he could find lucrative work and make money for their benefit.

Kalliope protested. The overwhelming empathy she felt toward her oldest son for having witnessed such a brutal double murder of his father and grandfather would solidify an even more profound connection to Plato, which she would carry with her as long as she lived. She couldn't dream of leaving him in Greece during his adolescence.

In addition, for practical purposes, she needed her eleven-year-old son to return with her so that he, too, could begin working right away. He was needed to help support the family now, not six or seven years into the future.

After many discussions over the months to come, Kalliope decided to leave her second son, John, in the care of his Uncle Kostas and Kostas's wife, Maria. This was the best compromise the family could come up with.

Six months after the murders, all four kids were still in a state of shock. John was unable to muster a protest. Tena and Jimmy, who were only eight and six years old, would block these memories out of their minds for life. Plato would never speak openly about what he witnessed that day, except perhaps to his wife. He would bury those memories deep within himself and move on with life like so many people did during that time.

Kalliope had to wait over a year after the murder of her husband and father-in-law before she could finally procure the paperwork and sponsorship to return to the United States. Of course, Kalliope's best friend, Chrissie, and Chrissie's husband, Alexander Hassapes, stepped up and helped sponsor her and her three children.

Family photo taken just prior to returning to the USA.
Notice how aged Kalliope looks to be after just one
year, compared to her passport photo. Notice the look
of anguish on Jimmy's face (left), the look of shock in
Tena's, and the "thousand-yard stare," of Plato (right).

John is absent from the photo, probably because he
had already gone off with his Uncle Kostas and Aunt
Maria to live in Salonika and begin his schooling.

Heartbroken to leave her son John in Salonika, Kalliope, with Plato, Tena, and Jimmy took the long journey to Pireaus on horseback and donkeys.

"Plato got the horse, and I got stuck with the donkey because I was the younger brother," Jimmy would joke decades later.

They boarded the SS *Leviathan* in the port of Pireaus on September 3, 1929, and embarked on another miserable voyage across the Atlantic. Nine days later, Kalliope would once again go through the immigration process on Ellis Island. This time, though, they ran into another problem. Records still existed that showed Kalliope had already immigrated to the States as a teenager and the authorities initially rejected her entry because of it.

Kalliope panicked. Having lived in the United States for quite some time before returning to Greece, her command of the English language was good enough to voice her protest. She explained her situation, how they originally returned to Greece the previous year for a "vacation," and how her husband was killed there. She also convinced the authorities that her children were American citizens. Based on her testimony and the family passport they still had in their possession from America, she was allowed processing and entry. The four of them breathed a sigh of relief as they boarded the train bound for Massachusetts.

Family portrait a couple years after they settled back
in Marlborough, MA. John is still absent in the
photo, living in Greece and plotting his escape.

CHAPTER 16

Independence Day

1936

John stood on the fourth-floor balcony of his Uncle Kostas's apartment. He gazed out at the ocean in front of him and thought to himself that this would be the last time he would take in this view. He wouldn't miss it.

For seven miserable years he endured physical abuse, mental torment, and neglect at the hands of his Uncle Kostas's wife, Maria. By the time he was thirteen, he had come to the conclusion that there was something mentally unstable with his aunt. He was convinced she had some sort of disorder and she couldn't help herself. At first he tried to be empathetic and sensitive to her condition, but that soon gave way to anger and resentment over his situation.

His siblings and his mother were living in the United States, in *his* hometown where he felt he should be. The letters he received from his mother were supportive and filled with love. She continually encouraged him to push onward and attain his high school education. She reminded him how his educational experience would be a great asset to himself and to the family. She explained that each of her boys needed to take on the role of "head of the household," now that their father was no longer alive. Each of her children had a role, she explained.

He closed his eyes and could imagine his older brother, Plato, and his younger brother, Jimmy, playing in the school band, taking tests in their Marlborough school and playing with the other boys in the neighborhood. He envisioned his little sister, Tena, playing in her room with her dolls and skipping rope on the street just a short walk from the factory where his mother worked during the day. He missed them terribly and with each passing day found himself feeling more and more distant from them.

"Listen to your Uncle Kostas and Aunt Maria," his mother would write. "They are so kind to take care of you and give you such a wonderful opportunity. Soon enough you will come back and live with us. We will be together again, I promise."

Kalliope had no idea how tormented John felt. His Aunt Maria censored every letter he wrote back. He was unable to share his feelings or reach out to his mother for help. Maria kept him locked up in his room when he wasn't in school. And Kostas certainly was no ally to John, either. He was just as much of an oddball, John concluded. The man was so focused on making money and staying clear of his wife's incoherent ranting that he simply couldn't be bothered with John's complaints. In his mind, his role as guardian ended with providing a home, food, and an education for the young boy.

"Just put up with it," Kostas would tell him. "She loves us both dearly and only wants the best for us."

Kostas was also often absent. His business dealings took him all over Greece. He visited their home village of Avgerinos from time to time, but John never wanted to go back. One time, Kostas and Maria insisted he come with them during the dedication and donation of an aqueduct Kostas made to the village in the name of his younger brother, Alexander.

"You have to be there," they told him. "We are donating this aqueduct in honor of your father and you need to represent your family."

John couldn't care less. He decided long ago that the moment he could remove himself from his deplorable situation, he would.

By the time he reached fourteen years of age, he began playing small pranks on his Aunt Maria just to get even for her treatment of him. She reached her breaking point one morning when she opened her dresser drawer, only to find a dozen dead frogs among her intimate undergarments. She locked him in his room for three days with little water and no food. His only reprise from his prison was the open balcony, four floors up, that overlooked the docks of Salonika.

John thought back on those three days as he stood on that very balcony now. He remembered yelling down, beckoning to the neighbors as they passed below him for some water or food. When the neighbors informed Maria, she retaliated this time with a belt. John couldn't sit down for a week. It would be the last time he would seek help from anyone again. He was alone in his sadness, alone in his suffering, and would be alone in his survival from this point onward.

But now John was seventeen years old. His schooling was over. He graduated with top honors from the private institution his uncle enrolled him in. Kostas had promised to send him back to America after graduation. John's excitement over the prospect of immediately leaving Greece the day after he finished school was immediately extinguished when Kostas informed him it would take about a year to get the paperwork together. He decided he couldn't wait that long. John fulfilled his promise to his family, and he was leaving his uncle and aunt as soon as he could.

John with his Uncle Kostas and Aunt Maria.

As he looked out over the ocean and at the ships coming in and out of the docks of Salonika, he secretly said goodbye to Greece and the horrors that he experienced there. From now on, his life would be lived on his terms. Never again would he be beholden to someone else's bidding.

"John," Maria called up to him. "Are you ready? Come down. It is time to go to church."

John stuffed what little money he had into the pocket of his suit. He left everything else on the counter, including his gold crucifix. Today he was not only walking away from his uncle and aunt. He was also leaving behind his religion.

What good did religion do me, anyway? he thought.

All the prayers and all the begging for God to help him out of his miserable condition and not a single prayer answered. It certainly didn't help bring his father or mother back to him. He knew the time had come to rely only on himself if he was going to make a life worth living.

He hurried down the stairs in the expensive suit Kostas bought him a year ago.

"You look handsome," Maria told him as she straightened his tie.

John didn't reply. He had no more words for this woman. He just stared back at her with a blank expression on his face.

After church services were over, and while his uncle and aunt were busy chatting with other members of the congregation, John simply slipped away. He walked out of the rear entrance of the church, down the street and toward the docks.

As he got closer to the docks, he noticed a long line of men waiting to be chosen to load a shipment of currants and cheese onto a small freighter. John looked around and noticed he was the best dressed person standing in line. He quickly removed his expensive jacket and laid it across a barrel as if he were hot and had intended to retrieve it later.

The foreman for the job, a gruff, middle-aged man started pointing randomly at the men.

"You, you, you, you, and you. You, you," and so on.

John wasn't chosen. It didn't surprise him. After all, John was small, young-looking, and very thin for his age. However, when the man next to him was chosen, John acted as if the foreman pointed to him instead and went with the man who was actually chosen, almost hiding behind the man in an attempt to blend in. Between the chaos of the process and the crowds of men going this way and that, it worked! John was in!

He immediately got to work like the other men in the hopes that the foreman wouldn't realize he had not chosen John for the day's loading. He noticed men with wheelbarrows standing in line, waiting for sacks of unknown items to be placed in them. He picked up the handles of one of them and wheeled it over to the line.

This is going to work, he thought. *It has to.*

After his wheelbarrow was loaded up with several sacks, he made his way over to the ship. His personal cargo was far heavier than he expected and he had difficulty maneuvering it into position in front of him to make his way up the gang plank and onto the deck of the ship.

As he pressed on and started up the incline, he feared there would be no way he could make it to the top. The load felt like it was getting heavier and he had no momentum. If he failed now, he feared the foreman would surely eject him from the docks and his plans, crushed. In reality, though, John had no exact plan. He was flying by the seat of his pants and making up his escape as he went along.

With every ounce of energy he could muster, he gave out a grunt and pushed the wheelbarrow up the gang plank and onto the ship. As he reached the top of the plank, the wheel dropped a good six inches down the step, off the lip of the hull and onto the main deck. John lost control of it all. The sacks fell to the side and he tripped forward and fell on top of them.

Without skipping a beat, several workers hustled over to him, picked up the sacks, threw them on their shoulders, and loaded them onto the large pallet, where they were to be secured with rope. No one reprimanded John. The foreman was too busy below on the docks to even notice what happened above him on the ship. One spilled wheelbarrow wasn't that big of an infraction for anyone to care.

He picked up the last sack, slung it over his shoulders and left the wheelbarrow off to the side where another dock worker retrieved it and took it away to be reloaded. Carrying the sack over to the rest of the cargo, he laid it down and then made himself appear to be busy as if looking for rope to help the other men tie the cargo down to secure it. John had a way of making himself look as if he knew what he was doing, even though he hadn't a clue.

All of that schooling, he thought, *and I don't know what it is to be a laborer like these men.*

On the other side of the cargo pallet, he found some rope and started fiddling with it, once again acting as if he knew what he was doing. It was then that he noticed the opening in the deck about twenty feet away from him. It was the hatch, and it was wide open. He walked over to the hatch as if it was part of the job, looked down, and could see stairs leading into the bowels of the ship. He took them and descended into the darkness.

Down into the hull he went. He made a right, then a left, then another left. He found more stairs and traversed deeper into the ship. No one was around. Everyone seemed to be on deck helping to secure the cargo. He opened a few doors and entered the dining area and kitchen.

This won't do, he thought. *Too much activity several times a day for meals. Gotta find someplace secluded.*

Eventually, he found his way to a large cargo hold in steerage. It was empty except for some empty pallets and a few crates scattered about. He immediately concluded it was perfect. He found a crevice behind some pipes and sat down. He thought about scavenging some blankets and food, but didn't want to take a chance of getting caught before the ship pulled out of dock. Instead, he tried to make himself comfortable.

John didn't know where the ship was going and he didn't care. He just wanted to get away from his uncle and aunt and away from Greece. He would live day to day and survive by his wits. As he sat there in the dark, he was immediately struck by the overwhelming sense of freedom. Here he was, hiding in the belly of a ship, heading toward a destination he knew nothing about with little money in his pocket and no companionship. Yet he relaxed for the first time all day and then fell into a deep sleep.

He was awoken a few hours later when he heard the ship's whistle blow. He could feel the ship move a little, and he knew he was on his way. Even now, he thought to himself, the ship would not turn around for a single unauthorized passenger.

Would the ship end up in another European country? Perhaps Asia or Africa or the United States? It didn't make a difference to him. Hours passed as John sat quietly in his crevice. He could hear footsteps above and people talking outside the door to the cargo hold several times. He didn't dare move. Not yet.

When the crew started quieting down, John estimated the time to be around midnight. Thirst and hunger began to overtake him. He had to get something to drink, at least. He waited another hour after hearing the last of the voices and footsteps of the crew, then quietly snuck out of the room and headed down the hallway toward where he remembered the kitchen to be.

Not a soul was to be found. John assumed everyone was asleep with the exception of whatever crew was navigating the ship. He entered the kitchen and found some water, which he guzzled with delight. He opened a few of the cupboards and boxes and discovered some bread, cans of fruit, and some jerky.

John stuffed what he could into his deep pants pockets. He then rifled through the utensil drawer for a can opener and a fork. Just then, he became aware that someone was watching him. He spun around, looked up, and saw a rather portly man standing in the doorway of the kitchen. John could only assume that the man must be the cook.

"What are you doing here?" asked the man in a semi-angry voice.

"I was just hungry for a midnight snack," John replied.

"Are you part of this crew?"

"Yes," said John. "I just couldn't sleep, so I came down here to get something to help with my hunger."

"Nonsense! I know every crew member aboard this vessel. I feed them all and I talk to them all. Tell me, boy, how old are you?"

John knew he couldn't lie his way out of this one. It was too late for any of the crew members to do anything about his trespassing now anyway, so he decided to come clean.

"I'm seventeen."

"How did you get on this ship, boy?" The cook's voice softened a bit. John could see that the man was trying to be kind and empathetic.

"I pretended to be a dock worker and I snuck on board. I needed to escape my home, and this was the only way I could think of."

"When was the last time you ate?"

"I haven't had a thing to eat all day, sir."

The cook smiled. His voice became softer. "Sit down. I will make you something to eat."

The cook prepared some leftovers for John and sat with him as he watched the boy engulf his meal. Then he took John to a crewman's quarters and showed him to a bunk that was not in use. John and the cook were quiet so as to not awaken the rest of the crew who slept on cots adjoining his. John hopped up on his cot, removed his shoes, and tucked himself under the single blanket.

"Get a good night's sleep, boy," whispered the cook. "In the morning I will take you to see the captain and you can tell him your story. Don't worry, the captain is a very nice man. I'm sure he will understand and have a solution for your problem."

John fell asleep listening to the sounds of the crew members' breathing and snoring. He had no idea where he was going or what was to become of him when he awoke. He just knew he was off on a journey that would take him into a new phase of his life.

The cook came in at 6:00 a.m. and woke up all the crew members, summoning them to breakfast. The seamen all looked perplexed as to who their new passenger was. Some of them rattled off questions to John.

"I'm a new crew member!" John said confidently with a wry smile on his face.

The crew laughed at this skinny little boy. John may have been just shy of eighteen years old, but he looked more like fourteen. He didn't take offense to the crew's laughter, though. He was happy to be among them. He hopped out of his cot as the crew dressed and got ready for their morning meal.

He sat among the crew during breakfast, but they didn't ask him any more questions. John listened to the crew's banter back and forth and was amused by it. When the meal was over, the cook came to collect him and brought John up to the captain's office. It was there that John told his entire story to the captain.

He recounted his life in America and how he was born in Marlborough, MA. He told the captain how his family immigrated back to Greece to live in their family village. He explained how just two months after being in Greece, his father and grandfather were beheaded by Albanian bandits and that his mother returned to the United States with his siblings while he had to stay behind to get his education under the care of a rich uncle and aunt.

He revealed to the Captain how, despite being enrolled at a very prestigious institution by his uncle, he was severely mistreated by him and Aunt Maria.

"They promised I would be sent back to the United States to live with my family when my education was finished, but when I graduated, my uncle informed me it would take up to a year to get the paperwork together to immigrate back to the States. I just couldn't wait that long. So, I decided I had to take matters into my own hands."

The Captain was immediately taken with the boy's story.

"Son," he said, "we need to get you back to your mother and your siblings in the United States. Our first stop is Athens. How about we go to the consulate together when we dock? I know some people in immigration there. Perhaps we can get you a passport so that you can be reunited with your family."

John hadn't even thought about that possibility. He was so focused on fleeing his aunt and uncle that he never even dreamed of being able to get back to the US to be with his mother and siblings. It had always been a fleeting, secondary thought to him.

"If you think that is possible, I would definitely be willing to try."

"Good," said the Captain. "Now, in the meantime, you must work on this ship. There are no freeloaders here. George," he said to the cook, "could you use another hand in the kitchen to prepare meals and clean up afterwards?"

"Absolutely," replied George.

When the rest of the crew came into lunch a few hours later, John smiled at all of them from behind the kitchen counter.

"See," he joked with them. "I told you I was a new crew member."

This brought the crew to laughter once more.

John spent the day shadowing the cook and helped him prepare and clean up after the lunch and evening meals. Instead of a drudgery, though, John found cooking to be quite enjoyable. He liked mixing together ingredients, serving the meals, and was drawn to the general organization skills it took to run a kitchen. He not only found the crew of the ship to be friendly and welcoming, but also found a passion for food prep as well. It was during his short time on this ship that he decided to make a career as a cook or as a chef. He chuckled at the thought that his family went through all the trouble of sending him to a top-notch school in Greece, and here he was contemplating the culinary arts as a livelihood.

When the ship docked in Athens, the captain took John to the French consulate while the crew unloaded its cargo and reloaded a new shipment.

"Why the French consulate?" John asked.

"Well, for two reasons," replied the captain. "First, it is where I have my connection," he said with a smile. "Second, we are heading to France in the morning. I thought you might want to come with us for the journey and we can part ways in Le Havre where you can board a ship bound for the United States there."

John was overjoyed. He couldn't believe the overwhelming generosity of this man. It had been a long time since anyone showed John the type of kindness this captain showed him now.

The Captain took him into the consulate and spoke with his friend there, who helped John attain a passport. *Jean Exarhopoulos* was written up on the document. It was the third spelling of his given name. Born Yiannis, anglicized to John, and now attaining the

French name of Jean. It was good enough for him. His photo was taken and stamped.

The two of them then went back to the captain's ship, where John helped loading the rest of the cargo, then went into the kitchen to help George prepare the evening meal. He was ecstatic and thankful at his turn of luck.

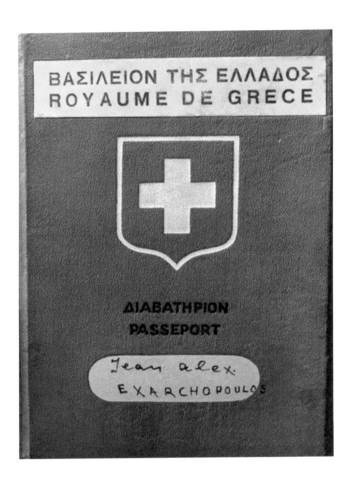

Three days later, the ship docked in Le Havre. The captain paid John for his services in the kitchen, then John said goodbye to the crew and thanked the cook and the captain. He spent almost all his money on a motel and meals for three nights and barely had enough to pay for his one-way ticket to New York City.

The following morning, on June 25, 1936, he boarded the SS *President Roosevelt*. Over the nine days it took to reach Ellis Island, John had a lot of time to think about his life; his past, his future. Although he never blamed his mother, the feelings he had harbored of his abandonment would never seem to go away. It was difficult to get over, and he never quite felt a true sense of connectedness to anyone as an adult. It was ironic, John thought to himself, that he was landing back in his native country, gazing upon Lady Liberty on the Fourth of July. It also happened to be John's birthday.

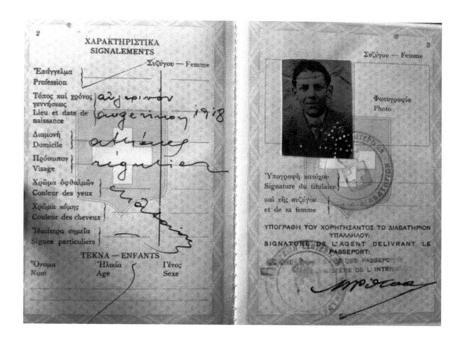

EPILOGUE

John's mother and his siblings were shocked and overjoyed when he showed up unannounced a month after passing through immigration. He avoided most questions about how he came to arrive in the States. He also preferred not to speak of his life in Salonika and the time he spent with his uncle and aunt. He simply smiled and showed off his new cooking skills by preparing family meals. He spent a little time with them and then moved on.

John married and stayed married for life and had two children. However, he was transient most of his adulthood. He hopped trains during the Great Depression and wound up cooking at various restaurants, diners, and cafés while on the road. He would show up unannounced to his own home and often at family functions, bearing gifts and stories of his travels. He would prepare the family meals for Christmas, Easter, and New Year's Day when he was around to celebrate them. By all accounts he had a heart of gold and was deeply loved by his friends and family. He just wasn't able to be present for too long.

Kalliope was considered a hero to the villagers, especially the children of Avgerinos. She earned so much respect from her extended family and friends there for her ability to pull herself together, go back to work in the shoe factory, and raise her three children on her own in the United States. She often sent care packages filled with clothing, candy, dolls, and toys for the children in the village. She also continued to send money whenever she could.

Plato and his youngest brother, Jimmy, were twelve and nine years old when the family returned to their home town of Marlborough. They immediately attained part-time jobs working paper routes, cleaning storefront foyers, and other odd jobs to help pay the bills and put food on the table. By the time Tena reached sixteen years of age, her mother pulled her out of high school to work in the shoe factory with her so that they could collectively make enough money to put Plato through college. Tena was distraught about having to leave school. Saddened by her situation and her desire to finish her education, her girlfriends would forever continue to invite her to their high school reunions even though she never graduated.

Plato, John, Jimmy, and Tena would all go on to have long, successful lives, lifelong marriages, and coincidentally, each would raise two children.

Alexander's descendants were not the only family members to be profoundly affected by his murder and the murder of his father. His siblings Pavlos, Yiannis, Vaia, and Soultana's lineages are pockmarked with descendants named after the family members who became murder victims, Alexander and Manolis. In this way, they have honored and memorialized their fallen ancestors.

The senselessness of the crimes is perplexingly poignant. Yet despite the tragedy and the brutal, emotional scar, each Exarhopoulos family member rose above it and led happy, successful lives while raising families of their own. Throughout the generations of grandchildren and great grandchildren, the family has passed down traditions of their Greek culture while keeping the murders a topic never to be fully discussed or explored, until now.

"Grandpa, what happened to your father and grandfather?"

Sitting quietly in his favorite recliner, Plato just looked down at his shoes. "They were beheaded."

BIBLIOGRAPHY

Information on the bandits and Markos Trimpos was drawn from the following sources:

1. Vasilis I. Tzanakaris. *Οι λήσταρχοι* (*The Bandits / The Brigands*). Athens: METAICHMIO Publications, 2016, pp. 431–445. http://www.biblionet.gr/book/
2. Gr. Har. Kandilaptis. "*Η ληστοκρατία στην Ανασελίτσα* (Bandit Rule at Anaselitsa)." Neapolítika, Issue 69 (Oct–Nov 2010), pp.15–20.
3. Nikos Fardis. "Δέκα μέρες με τους ασύλληπτους ληστές στα ληστρικά λημέρια και στις δροσόλουστες σπηλιές (Ten Days with the Elusive Bandits in the Bandits' Lairs and the Dew-Covered Grottoes)." Macedonia, (October 8th and 9th, 1928).

Information on the immigration process was drawn from several online sources:

1. Wikipedia. "Ellis Island." Retrieved October 2016. https://en.wikipedia.org/wiki/Ellis_Island
2. http://www.ellisisland.se/english/ellisisland_immigration1.asp
3. The Statue of Liberty Ellis Foundation, Inc. Retrieved October 2016. https://www.libertyellisfoundation.org/
4. Noelle, Talmon. "The Twelve Gruelling Steps to Immigration Through Ellis Island." Retrieved October 2016. https://www.ranker.com/list/ellis-island-immigration-requirements/
5. Oranger.com The Immigrant Journey http://www.ohranger.com/ellis-island/immigration-journey

Information about the Greek Orthodox Church in Marlborough, MA was drawn from their own website: http://www.stsanargyroi.org/

ABOUT THE AUTHOR

Jonathan Alexander Exaros has been a student of the martial arts since he was a young child and has taught thousands of students in New Jersey, New York and Pennsylvania since 1982. He is the owner and head instructor of a professional martial arts academy in Horsham, Pennsylvania, which has been in operation since 1991. His first book, "A Teacher's Inspiration: Methods of a Martial Artist" was written as a text book for his students and a means to enshrine and memorialize the teachings of his sensei. He is a graduate of Moravian College and is a lifelong student of history, philosophy, and religion. Jonathan is married and has two children.

Lightning Source UK Ltd.
Milton Keynes UK
UKHW050841050819
347380UK00005BA/17/P